WORK SHOP EAT

The Architecture of CORE

Introduction by Raul A. Barreneche

Edizioni Press

First published in the United States of America by Edizioni Press, Inc.
469 West 21st Street New York, New York 10011
www.edizionipress.com

ISBN: 1-931536-16-3
Library of Congress Catalogue Card Number: 2002107556

Printed in Italy

Design: William van Roden
Design Assistant: Alec Walker
Assistant Editor: Jamie Schwartz
Editorial Assistants: Sarah Palmer, Aaron Seward

MORE WITH LESS

Raul A. Barreneche

I first encountered the work of CORE when I lived in Washington, DC, on day-to-day walks through the city's uniformly bland, uniformly 12-story-tall canyons of office buildings. I was drawn to projects such as the Breadline bakery, Hannibal's coffee shop, and the Dean & Deluca food stores because their energetic modern style seemed startling among their environs. With little more than exposed concrete floors and columns and stained wood furnishings, Breadline and Hannibal's weren't flashy interiors. On the contrary, they were restrained and subdued. But there was something about their spare, modern character that signified more than an attempt at stylish, stripped-down minimalism. To me, CORE represented the desire to break from the status quo with simple and straightforward design, a real attempt to do more with less.

As I learned more about CORE's work, I discovered it wasn't limited to hip coffee shops and gourmet stores, to a single part of the city, or to a single building type. I found that some of their projects existed in prosaic settings that other architects would cast off as completely generic: shopping malls, airports, and suburban office buildings. Rather than be repelled by the generic quality of such environments, CORE let their spare, contemporary aesthetic transform the circumstances. In the Breadline, a fast-food-style bakery located on the ground floor of an anonymous office building near the White House, CORE stripped down the existing concrete structure to its essentials and added bare light bulbs, spare furniture, and few other flourishes to create an almost industrial space. The design is both noteworthy and economical—and it gives the store a strong identity with minimal means.

In fact, the Breadline is, in many ways, typical of CORE's work in that it underscores the firm's ability to use architecture to convey a client's identity with great economy. Both CORE and their clients realize that design, no matter how minimal, can communicate so much about a company if it is well considered: the nature of its business, how it stands apart from the competition, the image conveyed by its product. So many designers are concerned with creating memorable architecture through a surfeit of means, such as flashy materials or overpowering aesthetics. CORE prefers to create equally powerful design through the absence of expensive flourishes. Their spaces make both customers and budget-conscious clients quite happy, proving in the process that good design and good business sense doesn't have to come from costly, overly expressive architecture.

In many ways, CORE is deeply attuned to the commercial needs of its clients. They have realized that design can quickly and inexpensively build a strong brand identity, even for small clients with limited budgets. They have also recognized important growth areas and developed design services and solutions for businesses in these markets. Call centers, for example, are not the most alluring of building programs; most architects would write off these cavernous warehouses, where dreaded "customer service representatives" field telephone calls from unhappy customers, as lacking any possibilities for design. CORE has instead leapt at this kind of client and developed solutions that look to good design, clear thinking, and simple strategies to solve the job. CORE understands that their design solutions have helped call-center operators retain employees, despite the industry's notoriously high turnover rates. One can see how giving workers functional, well-designed environments, even within the boxy confines of a vast warehouse, would make all the difference in boosting employee morale and productivity—even though CORE couldn't completely do away with the box typology, nor with the repetitive nature of the work. We've been reminded that design can go a long way toward affecting psychological and behavioral changes.

Though decidedly modernist, CORE's pared-down sensibility is not alien to the genteel historic buildings that fill many of the neighborhoods of Washington and other older cities. The flagship Dean & Deluca store in Washington, for instance, is located within the nearly 200-year-old brick shell of the Markethouse, a prominent landmark in upscale Georgetown. Much of the firm's labor on this project involved behind-the-scenes operations: bringing the shell back to its original condition and seamlessly hiding the complex mechanical requirements of a vast, modern-day food emporium in the rehabilitated structure. They could then focus on creating a spare, streamlined interior that respected the historic shell and also conveyed the retailer's high-end, contemporary image. In another branch of the store, located beneath the historic Warner Theater in the old heart of downtown Washington, the architects took the opposite approach: Rather than hide the shop's inner workings, they exposed them, so as not to conceal the original structure.

CORE's design for the headquarters of the National Minority AIDS Council, located in a residential area of the capital, demonstrates a more aggressive approach to renovating and expanding historic buildings, in this case the signature brick townhouses that compose most of the city's housing stock. CORE preserved the exteriors of a pair of derelict townhouses and then expanded them with bold forms clad in corrugated metal. These additions aren't disrespectful of the original buildings; in fact, they convey a suitably colorful and optimistic feeling for a client with a serious task. And while one might expect conservative neighbors to fear such a bold design statement, they have instead embraced it as a positive beacon in a once-blighted neighborhood.

CORE's spirit of invention and their embrace of economy of means has helped the office grow by leaps and bounds, in a short time frame that would make many other practices green with envy. The firm's attitude, and the work that grows from it, not only sets the group apart from the competition in buttoned-down Washington, it makes CORE a model of business-savvy ingenuity throughout the country.□

OM

RK

PORTER NOVELLI

Washington, DC 1993

The Washington public relations firm Porter Novelli wanted their new offices to embody ideas of "interaction, dynamics, and neighborhoods." The company wanted the design of its space to reflect its innovative thinking and creative approach to developing programs.

CORE's solution was a linear arrangement with the company's creative and broadcast departments—its most dynamic elements—placed at opposite ends of the square, one-story space, which has a dog's head appendage. At the center of the linear arrangement is a reception area, furnished with an espresso bar and a TV, as well as conference rooms, a lounge, and access to an adjacent terrace. The coffee bar and lounge encourage interaction among staff, consultants, and clients.

The entire office is equipped with state-of-the-art audiovisual data and communications networks. Private offices are located along the linear corridors, which connect the creative and broadcast departments. When they are slid open, the four-foot-wide office doors, composed of maple frames with frosted panel insets, create a feeling of accessibility for inhabitants of the office and passersby. In fact, the entire office encourages interaction and communication, to reflect Porter Novelli's dynamic character.

The sleek modern design reflects the work of Porter Novelli's convergence and interactive marketing departments.

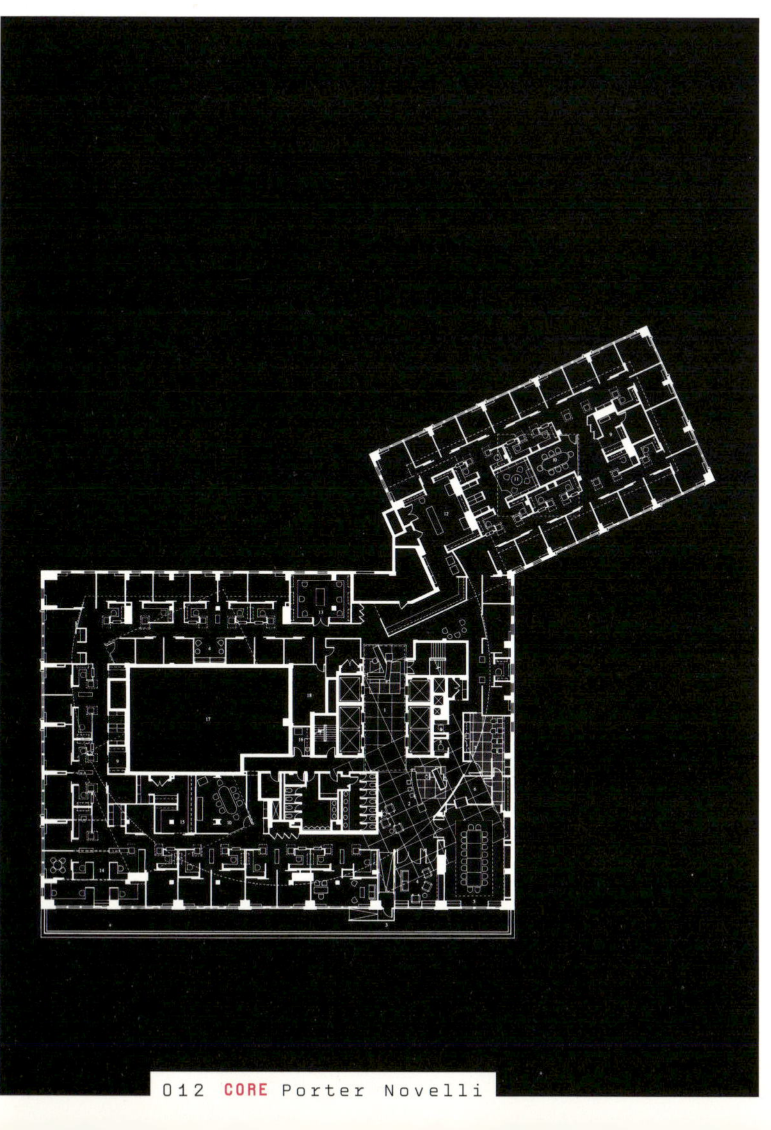

CORE counteracted a boxy floor plate with curving organic shapes within the design. Bright colors and plexi-glass bubble windows also help to create and open, fluid space.

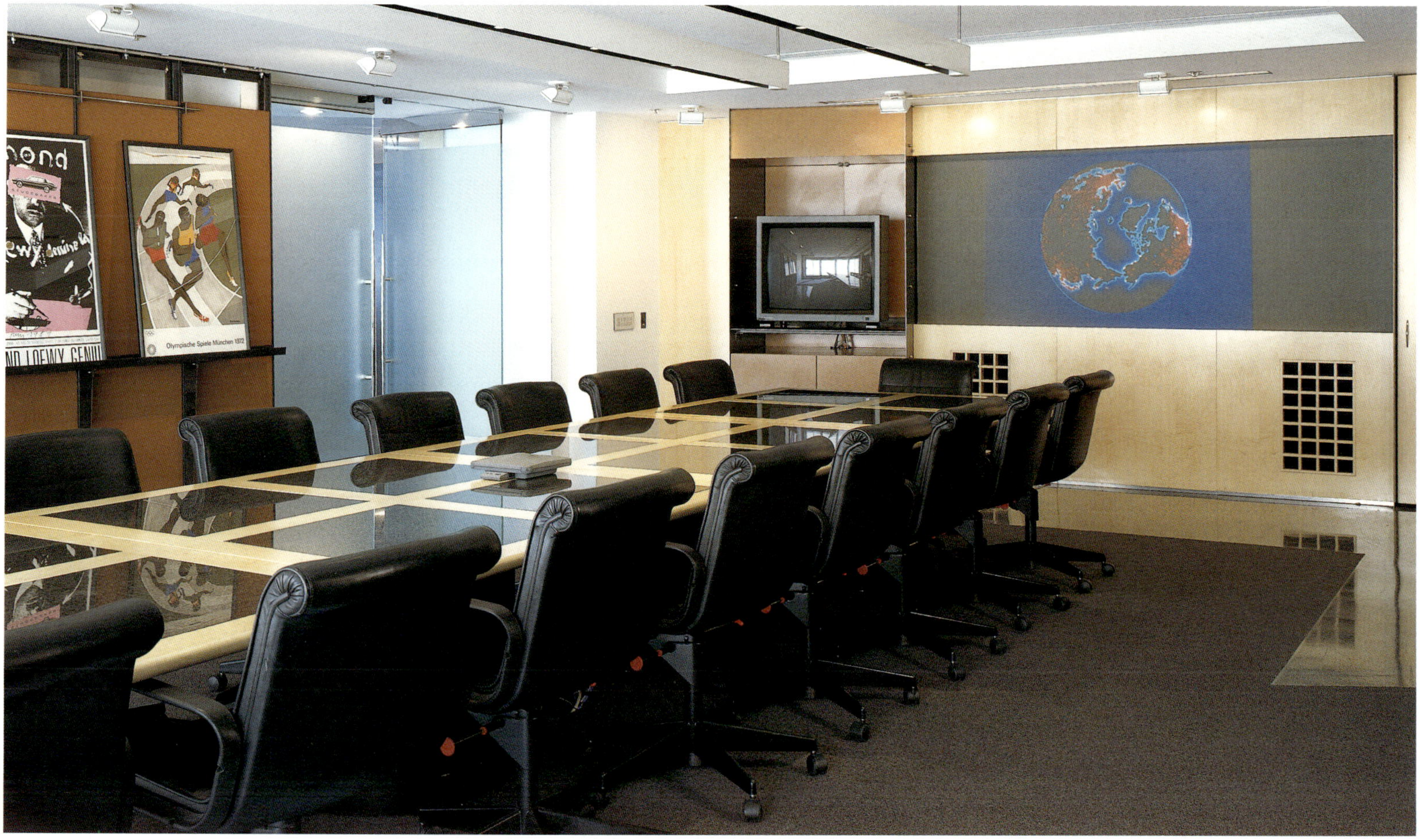
Olympische Spiele München 1972

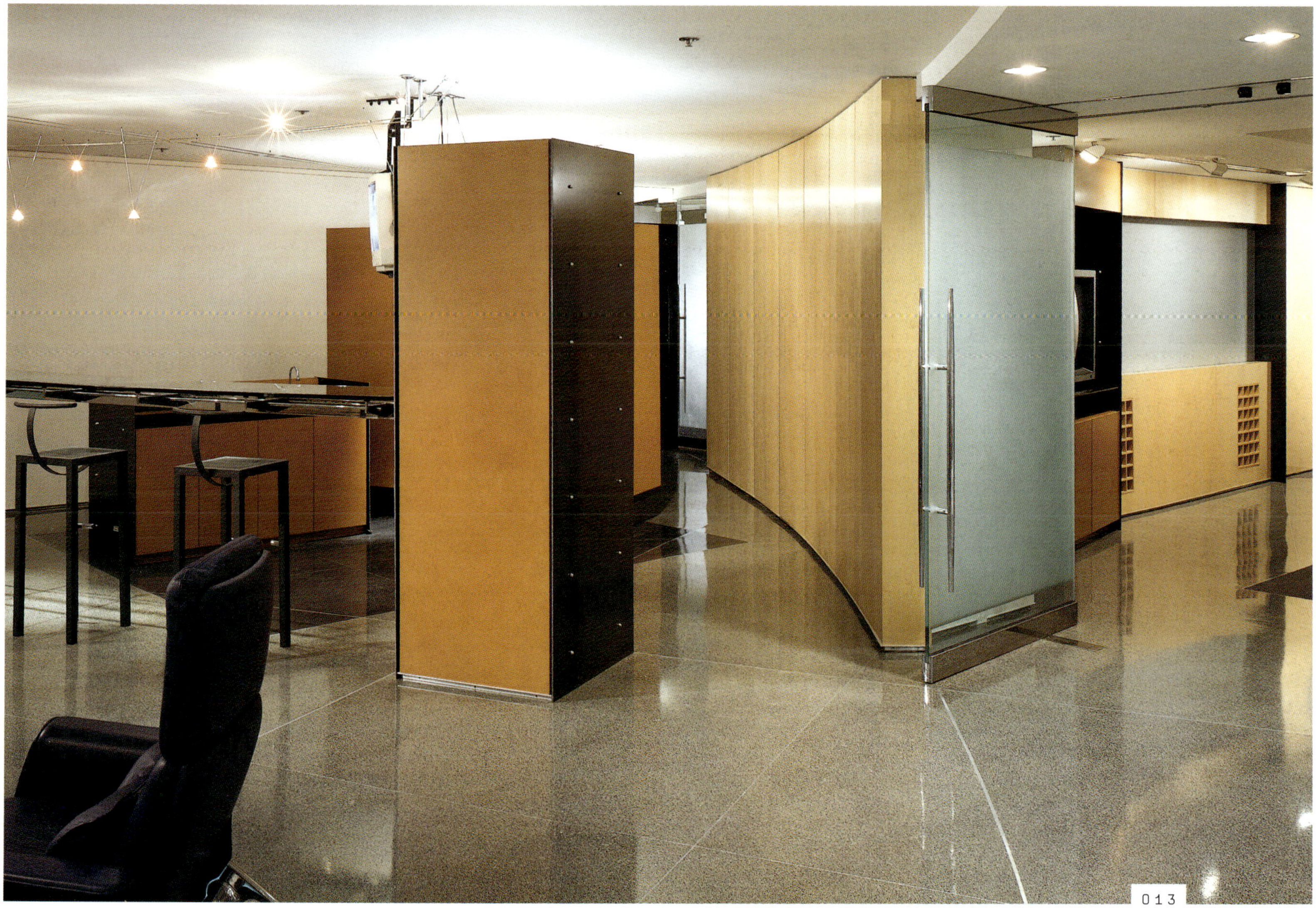

NATIONAL MINORITY AIDS COUNCIL

Washington, DC 1995

CORE designed the National Minority AIDS Council (NMAC) building as a monument to the victims of AIDS. The facility serves as the national headquarters for the AIDS organization, which has become the axis of all community-based organizations founded to fight the spread of AIDS and HIV. CORE converted two derelict, early 20th-century townhouses, located in a neighborhood destroyed by Washington's 1968 racial riots, into one large four-level building housing the offices and meetings rooms for a staff of 44.

CORE accommodated all of the required functions within a 7,500-square-foot site, on a tight budget of $700,000 for internal and external construction. They extended the building to its rear setback, added an exterior stair on the lower floors as a secondary egress, and inserted an elevator for the handicapped on the side of the building, rather than in the front. The brick building's original exterior was preserved and restored to represent the stability of an organization that deals with such an unstable disease. The addition, clad in galvanized metal panels, represents hope and future prosperity to AIDS victims as well as the surrounding community.

CORE approached the building's interior with the same concept of hope and optimism. Offices and meeting spaces promote group interaction and represent the belief that help can be found for those affected by the virus through the cooperation of many. For example, CORE separated the conference room and lunchroom with a removable sliding wall to create a large room that can be used for activities involving a large number of people. All desk surfaces, shelving, filing cabinets, and chairs were designed to maximize space and construction-dollar efficiency. Indigo-colored industrial carpet was used to give the space a contemporary feeling. CORE heightened this effect by punctuating the brick and metal walls with brightly painted wood panels and constructing a new back wall out of metal and glass, which wraps around parts of the side elevations.

The NMAC building was formerly two derelict townhouses located in a neighborhood decimated by Washington's 1968 race riots. CORE preserved and restored the original façade to represent the stability of this organization that fights AIDS.

CORE extended the building to its rear set-back. The new addition is clad in galvanized metal panels.

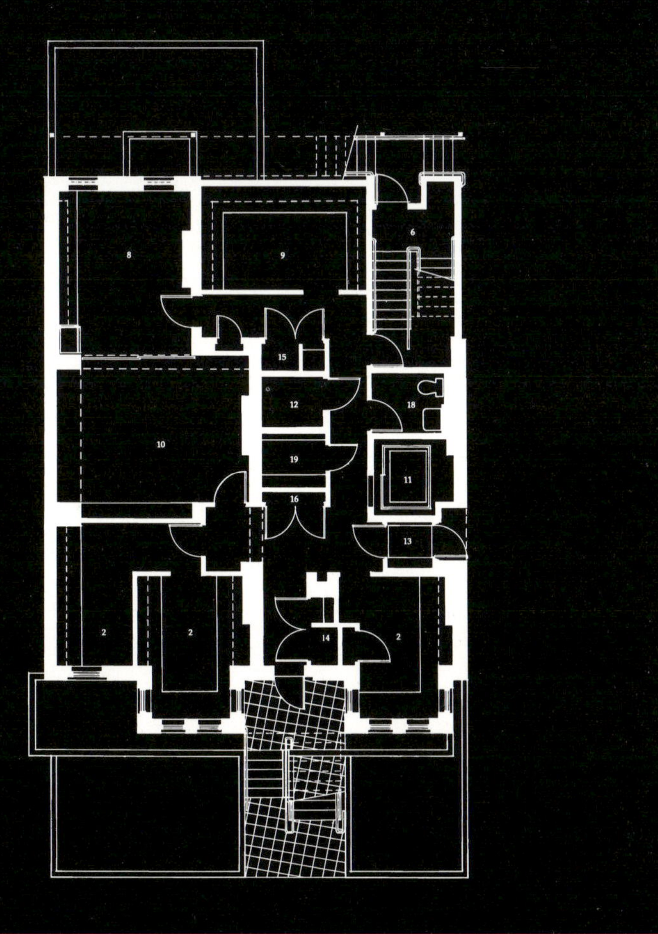

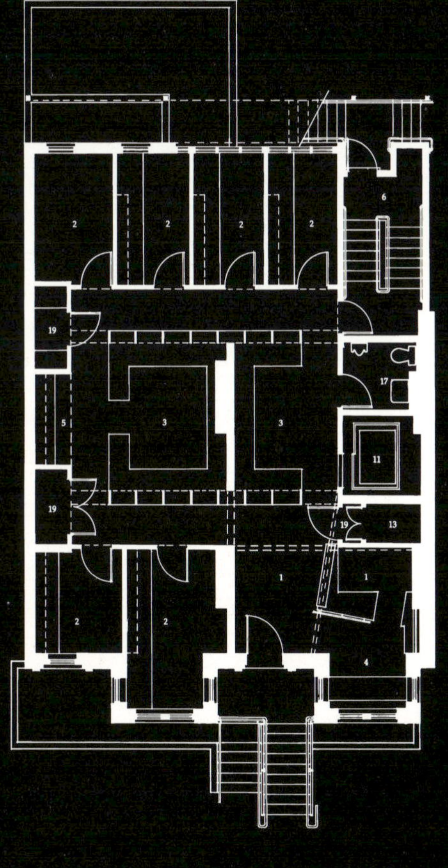

NATIONAL
MINORITY
AIDS
COUNCIL

CORE incorporated metallic finishes and bright colors to create an up-beat atmosphere. Indigo-colored industrial carpet modernizes the interior. All desk surfaces, filing cabinets, and chairs are flexible and cost-efficient.

SMARTEAM

Washington, DC 1998

As this graphic design firm began its fourth year of business, it was obvious that cramped office space was stunting the company's growth. When they first started the firm, the staff of four designers worked from a basement home office of about 400 square feet. By its fourth year, the firm had grown to serve important healthcare, education, and high-tech clients, so the staff expanded into a garage and bedroom. However, the firm rarely, if ever, allowed clients to visit their space, because it wasn't consistent with the high-quality work they produced; internally, the close quarters strained employee morale and affected the quality of their output.

The company scoured downtown Washington, DC, for bigger quarters that would reflect the modern style of its work and employees. It had to be a unique, convenient, inviting, playful, and functional space. They struck gold on U Street with a 2,100-square-foot vacant warehouse loft (formerly a Chrysler dealership), with exposed pipes, distressed brick walls, cement floors, and a freight elevator. CORE shared the client's enthusiasm for the potential of such raw space.

CORE faced three major challenges: to create a functional space evocative of the "high design" produced by the firm; to celebrate the character and rough patina of the existing space; and to work within an extremely tight budget. CORE met the challenges with a variety of innovative solutions. They established three distinct elements that define the space. The functional areas, including the copy machines, storage facilities, and pantry, feature a maple and steel wall defining one edge of the president's office. The second element is composed of workstations constructed from inexpensive birch veneers and heavy-duty sliding door hardware, instead of standard cabinet hardware. The final element is a series of colored burlap curtains, which provide sun control at the perimeter and create a soft figural wall when paired with the last anomalous element—a steel oil drapery.

CORE renovated a 2,100-square-foot warehouse loft to accommodate a graphic design firm. Pared down materials reflect the company's modern work. Workstations are constructed of inexpensive birch veneers and heavy-duty sliding door hardware.

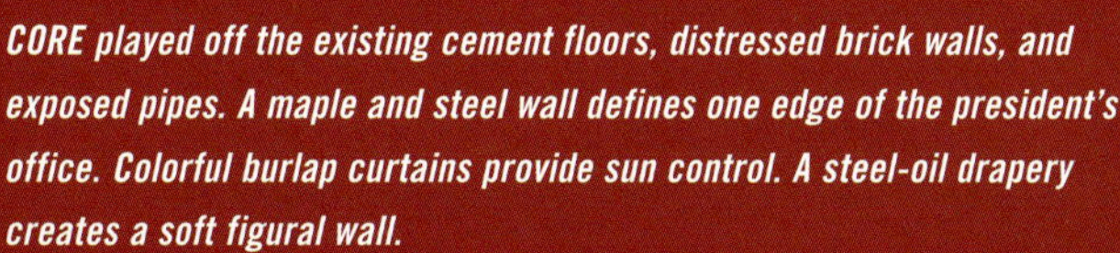

CORE played off the existing cement floors, distressed brick walls, and exposed pipes. A maple and steel wall defines one edge of the president's office. Colorful burlap curtains provide sun control. A steel-oil drapery creates a soft figural wall.

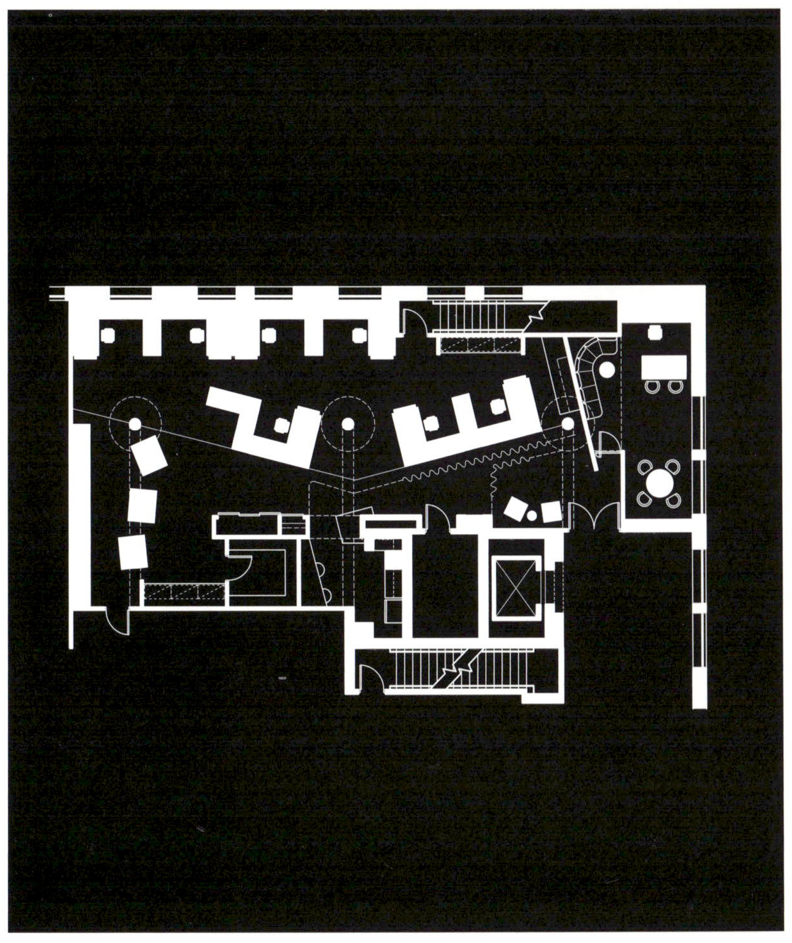

N.E.W.

Great Falls, Montana 1998

This call center in Montana was the client's first satellite facility outside its Northern Virginia headquarters. The client wanted to create an employee-friendly environment that would nurture happier telephone customer service representatives, given the grim fact that the average employment term for these kinds of employees is only six months. The high turnover at most call centers is due to a complete lack of privacy and a clinical, sterile work environment. The client and CORE agreed that happy employees are more productive; they view their jobs with a higher regard and are less likely to leave. CORE believed an atmosphere that was relaxed, positive, and fun, yet technologically sophisticated and responsive to customers, would help keep employees. The client agreed, but also wanted to take things one step further by adding unexpected amenities for this 24-hour call center, housing roughly 300 employees on the second and third floors of an existing windowless building.

CORE created a new entry, added an elevator to the second and third floors, punched new windows into the building's solid skin, and added a long, 200-sqaure-foot balcony and skylights on the building's west side. Offices of varying sizes and heights are grouped along the perimeter of the space, while the center contains open workstations for telephone representatives and claims adjusters. An elevated supervisor's tower has visual but not physical access to the adjacent computer room. The design also includes perks for the employees: a training room, a workout facility with showers, and a generous kitchen and break room.

CORE concentrated on lines, planes, and volumes to generate three-dimensional layering within the building's envelope. These elements interact with each other to create vistas and natural gathering spaces. The creative use of an extremely simple but bold palette of carpeting, painted drywall, and concrete gives vitality to the space.

The goal of boosting the company's spirits and employee satisfaction, productivity, and retention has worked, thanks to the optimistic design of the space and the new opportunities for enhanced interaction and communication it creates.

CORE took on the challenge of designing an employee-friendly customer service call center. A new entry clearly announces the presence of N.E.W. to passersby and establishes the open, accessible atmosphere the designer sought to create.

N.E.W.
N.E.W. NATIONAL ELECTRIC WARE

CORE organized open workstations in the center of the plan, while locating
private offices and training rooms of varying sizes at the perimeter of
the space. A combination of direct and indirect lighting creates is appropriate
for the below-grade facility.

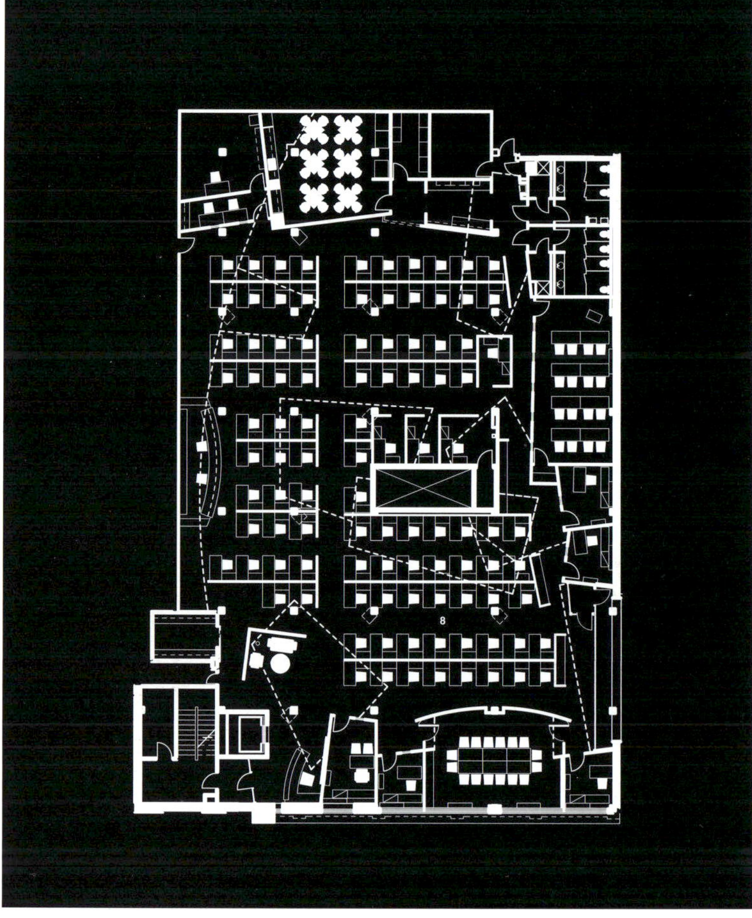

The interior design promotes a relaxed, positive, fun environment for employees. A simple, bold interior palette includes carpet, painted drywall, and concrete. Shifting ceiling and wall planes create visual interest. *CORE* also incorporated amenity spaces, such as a generous kitchen, in order to help reduce employee turnover.

BBC AMERICA

Bethesda, Maryland 1998

The British cable television operation BBC America, a branch of the venerable British Broadcasting Corporation, wanted what many corporations seek from their architect: a lot of bang for few bucks. BBC America asked that its 8,700-square-foot offices in suburban Washington, DC, be open and visually appealing—and economical. CORE responded by renovating existing offices into a space with the feeling of a television soundstage.

The program required editing rooms, meeting areas, an equipment hub, and flexible workstations for the production staff. The mechanical infrastructure was to be upgraded to provide individual air conditioning units for each of the edit rooms and equipment areas. To keep costs down and make the addition of broadcast equipment easy and visually unobtrusive, CORE revealed most of the raw construction materials. They backed high-gloss laminate panels with exposed metal studs, raw steel, and plywood. They also painted the raw concrete floors, creating a combination of jewel tones with smooth and textural surfaces. Low partition walls produced the open feeling of a soundstage and reinforced the client's office culture of easy communication and interaction. The finishing touch was sleek but affordable furniture from the Swedish retailer IKEA—the perfect solution for a design based on simplicity and style on a budget.

At the reception area, CORE established the interior palette of high-gloss laminate panels backed with exposed metal studs, raw steel, and plywood.

BBC AMERICA
SONY

The design includes flexible workstations that maintain the office culture of easy communication and interaction. The interior reveals raw construction methods, and provides an appropriate backdrop for broadcast equipment. Sleek IKEA furniture compliments the design.

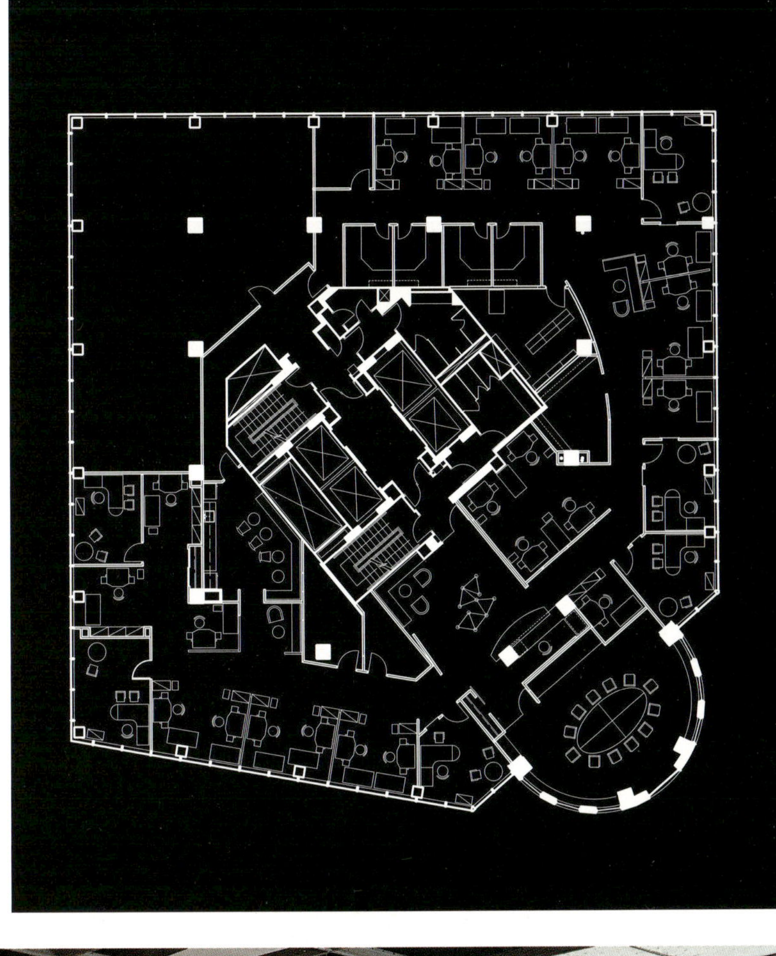

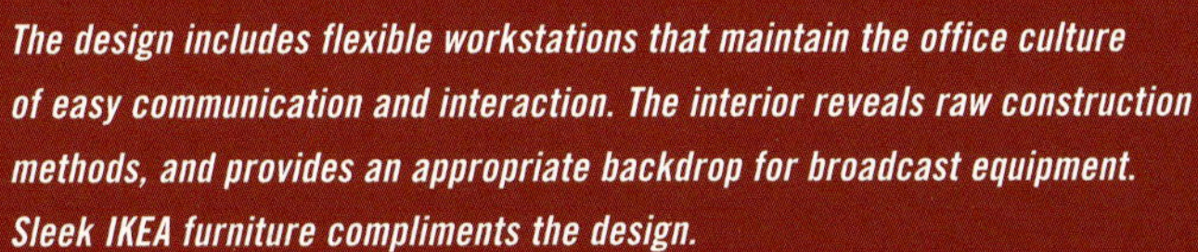

BBC AMERICA
SONY
SONY

A&E

San Antonio, Texas 1998

This customer service call center for electronic warranty coverage and claims seats 125 operators who respond to inquiries about product warranties. The center, which operates 24 hours a day, seven days a week, is a difficult new building type. The highly competitive industry requires a significant investment in up-front employee training—but high employee turnover is a common problem, due to corporate policies, lack of benefits, and bad working environments. This client's demands were complex: a building that would attract the best employees, reduce turnover rates, and keep labor costs down.

CORE abandoned the large "white box" of cubicles—the typical model for most call centers—while working under an extremely tight budget. Instead, CORE developed an unconventional "out of the box" design with a strong visual character by organizing basic materials in unusual ways. To keep costs down, CORE built the new center within an existing prefabricated metal warehouse in an inner suburban industrial park near downtown San Antonio. They repainted the building's corrugated metal exterior and designed an exterior wood deck as a retreat for smokers. Inside, they removed the existing ceiling to expose the sloping steel roof structure and installed exposed-lamp fluorescent fixtures upside down on the ceiling to create cheap but efficient indirect lighting; simple galvanized-steel shields on the fixtures reflect additional light upward onto the ceiling. New windows allow a measured amount of natural light into the computer-intensive environment.

CORE located help-desks, where operators man the phones, in centralized spots within the L-shaped plan and pushed training rooms, offices, conference rooms, break rooms, and support rooms to the perimeter. They strategically located elevated "towers," where supervisors can work and monitor all help-desk personnel. These "towers" are constructed of exposed-edge birch plywood with plastic laminate work surfaces; translucent sheets of structural plastic provide some privacy for the supervisors. Plastic sheets also act as interior windows for offices, conference rooms, and training rooms, which are defined by walls of varying heights and colors.

The help-desks were built on site from solid-core birch veneer doors and medium density fiberboard (MDF). These workstations are organized along low partition "spines" made of simple drywall, with MDF cable trays placed along their tops to organize voice and data cabling. Each workspace is sparsely but efficiently equipped with an ergonomic chair and keyboard tray, a pencil drawer, and a task lamp. The placement of the desks encourages the formation of individual teams, once again boosting productivity through commonsense, economical means.

Cheap, but effective lighting consists of simple suspended halogen fixtures and exposed lamp fluorescent fixtures installed upside down.

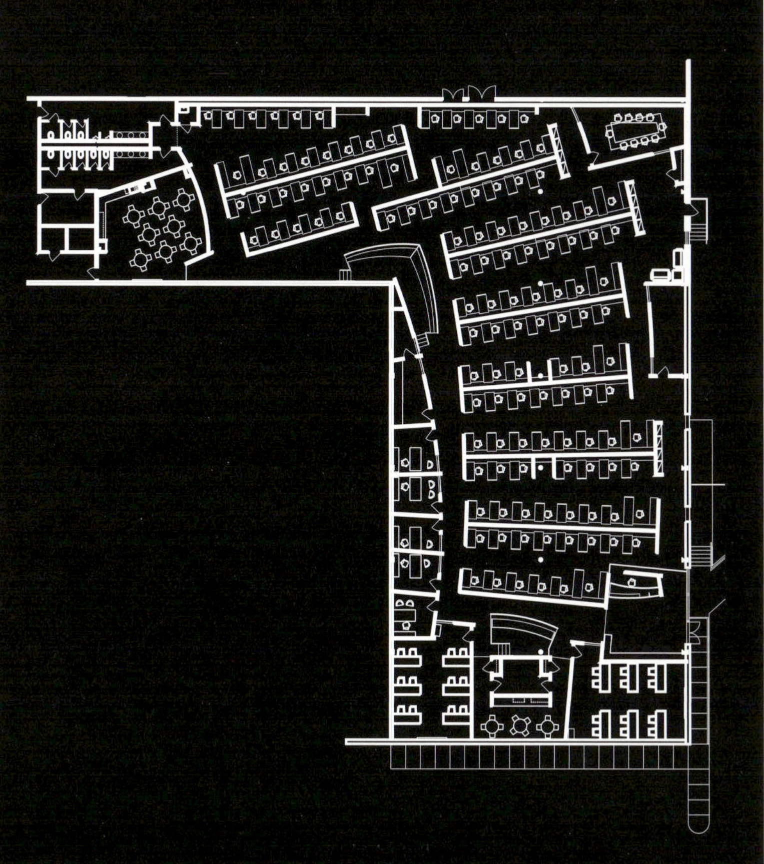

CORE organized help-desks at centralized locations within the L-shaped plan. Workstations are organized along low partition spines that also house voice and data cabling. CORE removed the existing ceiling to expose the sloping steel.

E-SYNC

Trumbull, Connecticut 1999

CORE created a subdued, state-of-the-art facility that gives clients of this electronic mail-routing network provider a sense of security, while creating an environment that showcases the company's creative network solutions. The client selected an unusual site: a building in a technology park with 17,655 square feet of below-grade space, which was originally constructed for a defense contractor. CORE's challenge was to create functional and inviting spaces in this windowless underground facility.

Since there were no windows, CORE focused on the interior space, redirecting vistas from outside to inside. They carved the internal spaces to take advantage of the 20-foot-high ceilings, establishing offices of various heights and sizes along the perimeter of the space. The design divided the facility into marketing and technical zones, using the original physical boundaries. This disjointed and layered design produced the functional space desired by the client and resolved the client's security concerns by restricting access to specific areas.

CORE utilized color in the carpeting as directional cues: blue designates the north-south axis and aqua designates the east-west axis. The colors also identify key points of circulation and reorientation.

CORE reserved the central core for workspaces equipped with storage light towers, columns that house compact fluorescent fixtures and reflective vinyl panels to redirect light to work surfaces. Open spaces between the workstations feature comfortable seating and colored marker boards to encourage team interaction. This use of space creates a unique interior landscape where nothing aligns, but the disorder is functional. Everything must be in a specific non-linear position for the facility to function.

CORE also developed horizontal layering features to balance the vertical layering of spaces, using glass and open space to visually span physical separations. In addition, this layering allows multiple functions to be seen from a single location. CORE balanced their arrhythmic approach with recurring themes and design elements, in keeping with the client's goals.

The reception area introduces a palette of colors and materials that CORE uses throughout the office.

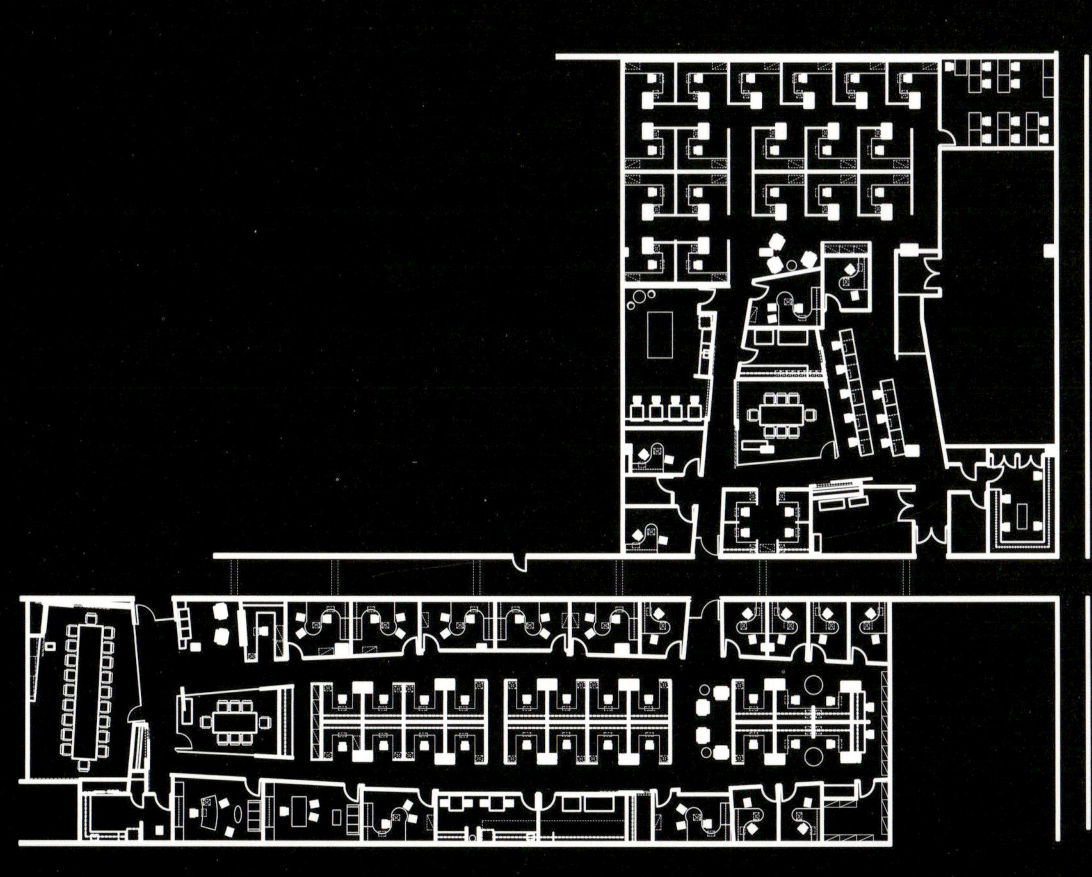

CORE carved vistas out of the windowless space to create a dynamic, expansive environment. Features such as slanted and shifting wall and ceiling planes, half-height walls, exposed ceilings, and glass partitions prevent the space from becoming stuffy and allow views across the office from multiple locations.

CATHOLIC CHARITIES

Washington, DC May 2001

Catholic Charities is a regional philanthropic organization that provides social and legal services to the Washington Metropolitan community. In 1999, the organization decided to move from its small 20,000-square-foot facility in a converted supermarket to a 100-year-old, 30,000-square-foot former parish school in downtown Washington, DC. Four floors of the eight-floor building would accommodate community training facilities, as well as offices for 50 staff members. CORE renovated the 19th-century building to accommodate a 21st-century social services facility.

The challenges of the project were formidable, but CORE utilized the building's inherent attributes to create an appropriate design. For example, they exposed the existing load-bearing brick walls to give character to the interior spaces. The building's unusually high structural clearances allowed for expansive, airy spaces that take full advantage of natural light through the large existing windows. CORE mitigated the potential pitfalls of large, open work areas by introducing details such as a skewed column grid that follows the central circulation path, abstract trellises that tie the column grid together, and lighting fixtures that bring down the overall scale of the space.

The workstations are typically clustered along the west window wall. They consist of a basic drywall enclosure of various heights with millwork counters and built end overheads. The stations also contain files, mobile pedestals, task chairs, and task lighting. The design includes some enclosed 10' by 10' and 10' by 15' offices on the upper floors along the east window wall for employees that require privacy. Training facilities, where the staff works with members of the community to improve their technical skills, are located at the basement level. The training areas include flexible tables to accommodate a variety of activities.

The owner of the school building, St. Patrick's Parish, is allowing Catholic Charities to occupy the building for 20 years, so the designers focused on durable materials. Selective application of lasting and dynamic materials, such as stained MDF and painted steel plates, convey an impression of practicality and compassion that is appropriate for the organization. Various natural and artificial light sources create the desired balance and feel.

The entryway reveals the building's former use as a parish school.
CORE maintained existing details, weaving them into the new design.

CATHOLIC
CHARITIES

FAITH
WORKS
WONDERS

The renovation accommodates community training facilities, as well as offices and amenities for 50 employees. CORE prevented the renovation from creating large, undefined work areas by introducing details such as a skewed column gird that follows the central circulation path, abstract trellises that tie the column grid together, and lighting fixtures that minimize the overall scale of the space.

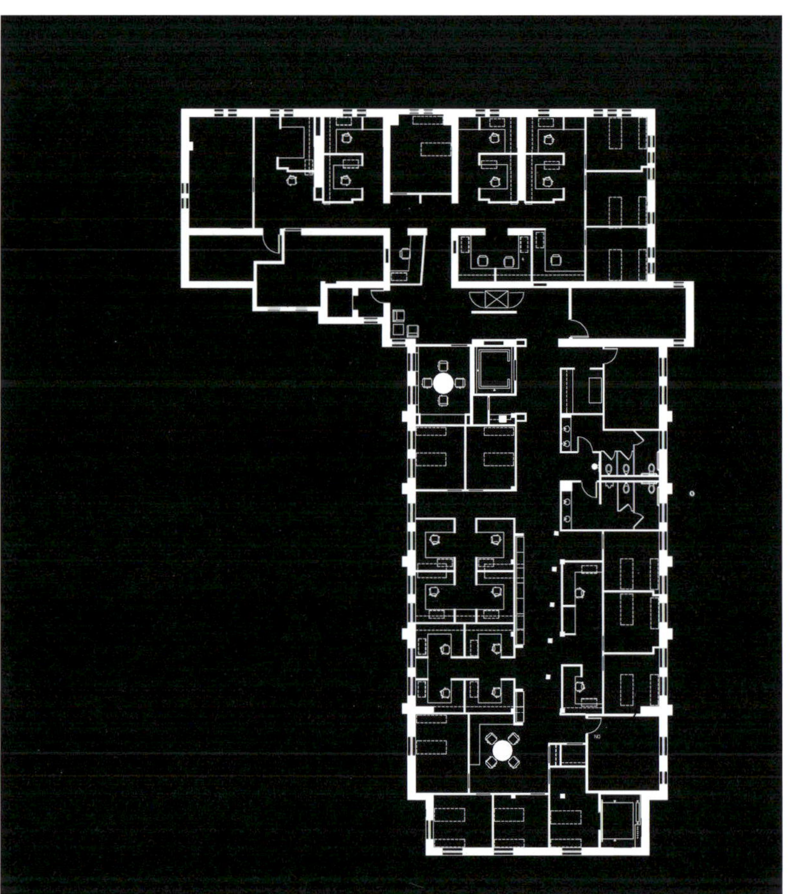

PORTER NOVELLI: INTERACTIVE

Washington, DC 2001

Porter Novelli asked CORE to design a new space for their Convergence & Interactive marketing departments within their existing office building in downtown Washington, DC. The space had to reflect the group's creative personalities and support their shifting operational needs. CORE was challenged to create a design that would parallel designs CORE had executed for the company seven years earlier.

CORE responded by designing a set of loosely arranged spaces defined by curved drywall walls within the rigid, boxy floor plate. The assemblage of organic volumes is rendered in planes of saturated colors: bright green and blue contrasted by orange edges. CORE also incorporated glass at the entry and plexi-glass bubble windows throughout the space to maintain an open, light-filled environment. Where the original space was rigid and neutral, the new design is fluid and vibrant.

The new space accommodates the latest technology, while maintaining creative flexibility. Modular furniture systems and movable wall panels allow the employees to rearrange the office. Work areas can expand or contract as necessary to accommodate the groups' varying tasks and moods.

The elements of the design—the energetic color palette, movable furniture, slender fluorescent tube lighting and spot lighting, and highly-textured spray-on acoustic ceiling—express Porter Novelli's innovative and energetic culture.

CORE incorporated transparent doors and circular portals to create an open atmosphere and encourage collaboration within this dynamic office.

PUSH

The entire office is equipped with state-of-the-art technical systems, but
CORE prevented the space from becoming too alienating by adding
whimsical details, such as portal windows and four-foot-wide office doors
that can be slid open to create accessibility.

*CORE established a linear organization for the one-story space, with
its dogshed appendage. The corridors connect the creative and broadcast
departments, which are located at opposite ends of the plan. In the
center of the office are the conference rooms, a lounge, and access to
an adjacent terrace.*

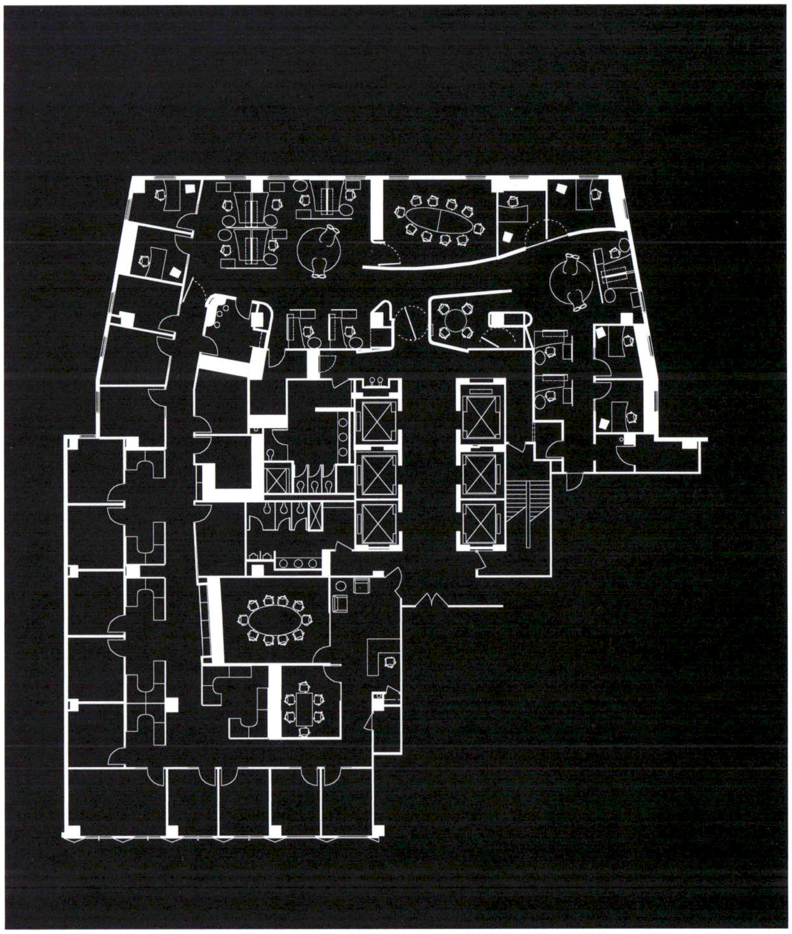

OUR WORLD
SH

OP

PROFUMI

North Bethesda, Maryland 1994

CORE has long been curious about the inspiration behind so-called "impact retail." Its principle is simple: to make people feel compelled to enter a shop by creating an environment that conveys the essential qualities of the products sold there. In the case of Profumi, a perfume shop in suburban Washington, CORE's design couples the senses of sight and smell to create the same atmosphere of romance and desire that compels consumers to buy perfume.

CORE used traditional craftsman's techniques to create a fresh, crisp space. The shop features wrought-iron display pedestals crowned by glass cases filled with merchandise. Illuminated boxes exhibit the jewel-like perfume containers. The hand-forged steel supports of the wall fixture are sensuously curved. Crisp oak millwork underscores the shop's sleek aesthetic. CORE dressed the walls in powdery shades of purple, blue, and aqua to offset the amber and yellow perfume bottles. The broken mosaic tile floor pattern suggests the swirls of the ocean and the warm colors of the sky and sea.

CORE's design of the initial store established an overall image for this up-start company. Other locations will be built following CORE's original design, which includes adaptable elements such as modular display cases that can fit the configuration of future stores.

CORE's bold design created a distinct image for this upstart company and established basic design themes, which can be used at other locations.

EXIT

CORE used details, such as a powdery pastel palette, a broken mosaic tile floor, and sensuously curved millwork, to express the essence of perfume and draw passersby into the store.

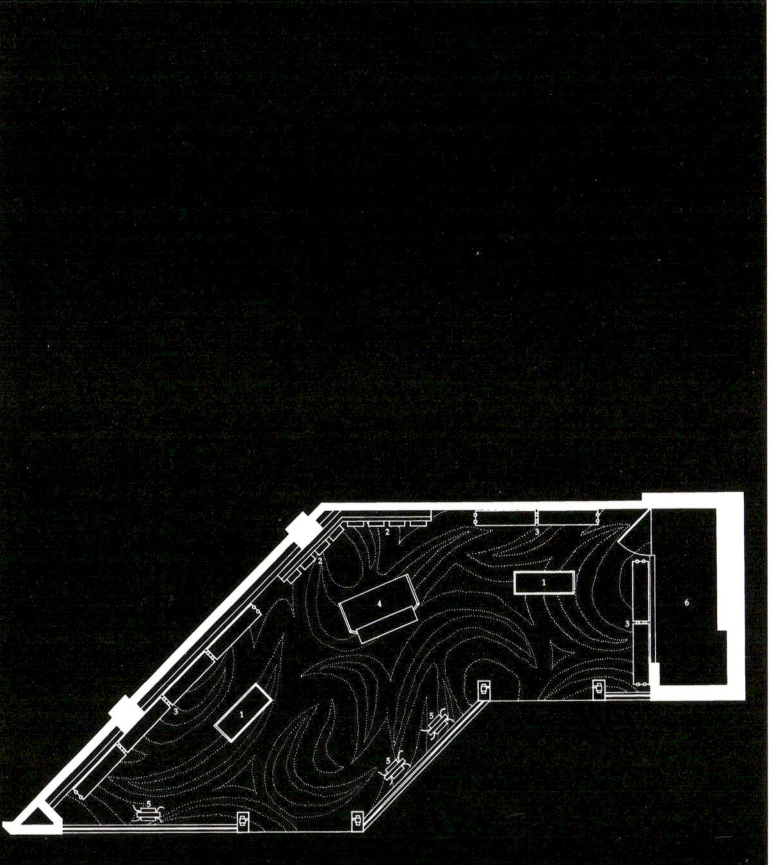

APC/SPRINT PCS STORE

Washington, DC 1995

CORE was instrumental in launching three digital wireless stores for Sprint Spectrum, a new digital communication technology developed by American Personal Communications in a joint venture with Sprint PCS. The clients' goals were to educate the public on the advantages of digital technology, as well as to sell products and accessories, such as phones and headsets. CORE designed a 5,500-square-foot flagship store in downtown Washington, DC, in less than seven months.

Mobile telephones and service plans are sold on the sales floor, which is located to the right of the street entrance; a customer service area, where customers can pay bills and have equipment serviced, is located to the left of the entry.

CORE created a racetrack configuration that incorporates the sales, activation, purchase, and service areas; though the areas are all connected, they remain separate and distinct. An oval kiosk at the center of the racetrack, ringed by mobile phones mounted on holders and stools for customers who want to speak with a representative, houses sales personnel and product samples. By placing sales staff in the racetrack, the plan allows customers to explore the rest of the store without being overwhelmed by salespeople.

The area surrounding the racetrack focuses on the display of digital wireless phones and accessories, as well as interactive video displays that explain the advantages of digital wireless technology. There are also racks filled with product literature, big screen monitors, comfortable seating, and a refreshment bar, which allow shoppers to learn about Sprint's products in a relaxed environment.

CORE created private offices for the store manager and the customer service manager near their respective service areas. Across the hall are a room for communication and computer equipment and a tech room, where more complicated testing and repairs take place. An opening through which handsets can be given to technicians is located off the hallway.

The finishes—a combination of warm woods such as maple, anigre, and cherry wood and more high-tech metal surfaces—convey an air of lightness and openness throughout the store. A colorful, back-lit map detailing the coverage area of Sprint Spectrum's services dominates the shop's rear wall, while a Mecco Shade fabric painted as a cloud-filled sky, floats over a recessed ceiling.

Warm woods and high-tech metal surfaces create a comfortable atmosphere. A mecco shade fabric painted as a cloud-filled sky floats over a recessed ceiling, adding a bit of whimsy to the design and enlivening the experience for shoppers.

System Demonstration

CORE established a race-track configuration, which connects sales, activation, purchase, and service areas. Sales staff remain inside the race-track, allowing shoppers to explore the store in a relaxed environment. Screen monitors let shoppers learn about the products on their own.

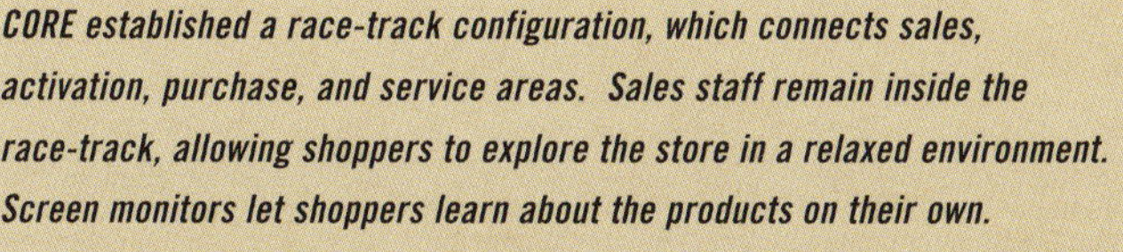

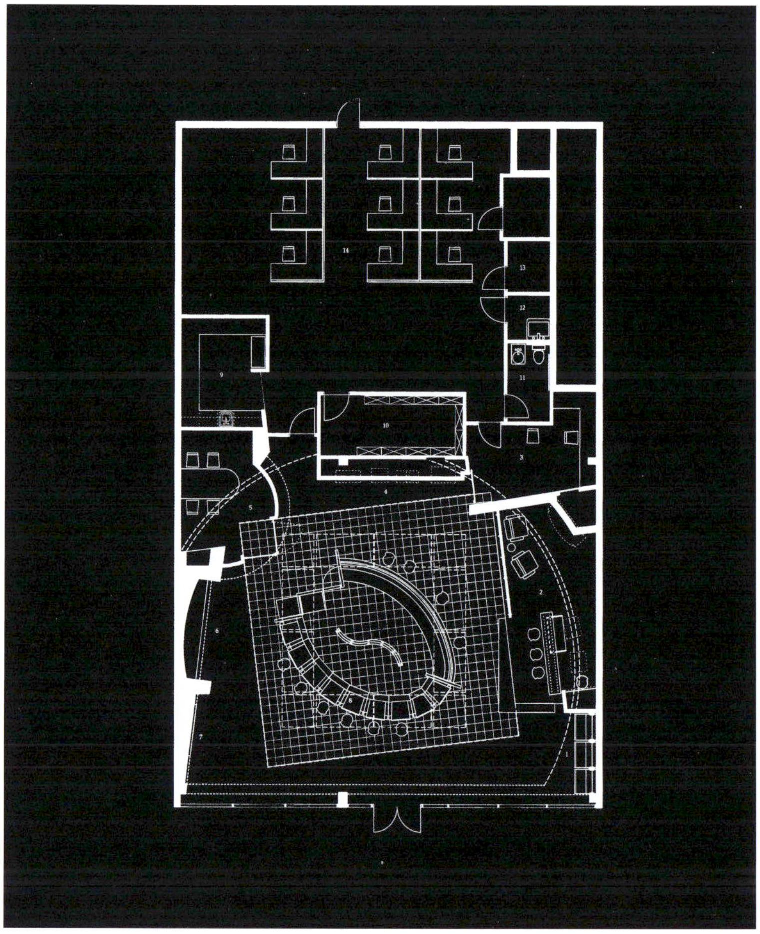

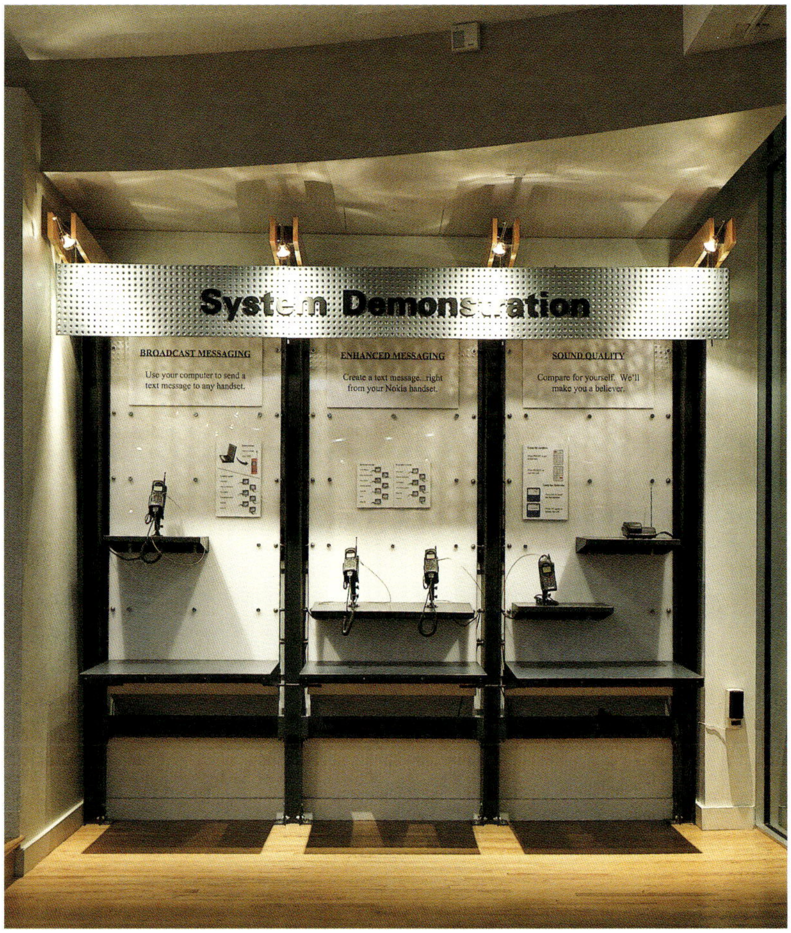
BROADCAST MESSAGING
Use your computer to send a text message to any handset.
ENHANCED MESSAGING
Create a text message...right from your Nokia handset.
SOUND QUALITY
Compare for yourself. We'll make you a believer.

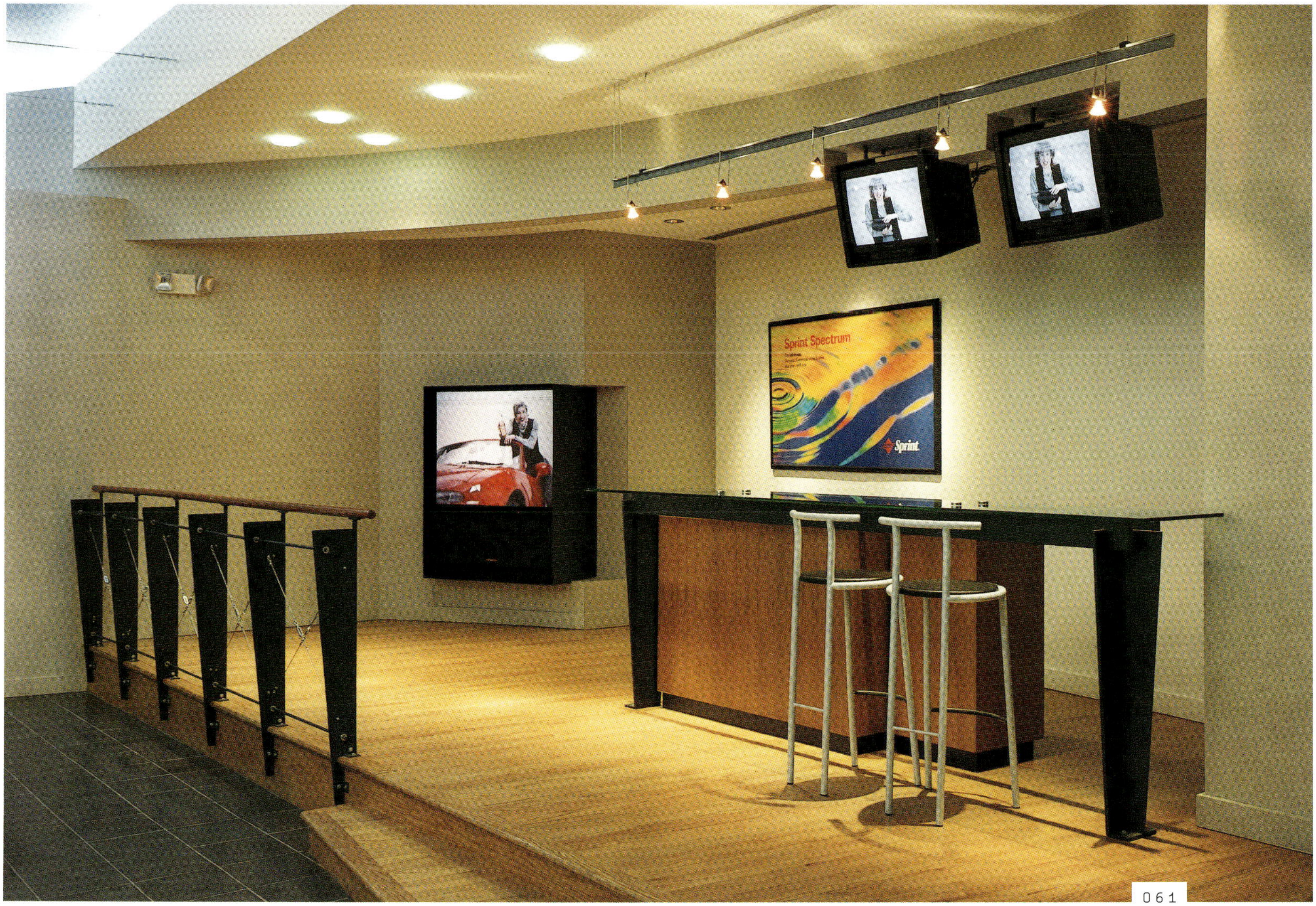
Sprint Spectrum
Sprint

DISCOVERY CHANNEL STORE

Pittsburgh, Pennsylvania 1997

Discovery Channel stores, an outgrowth of the cable television channel, provide consumers with a compelling mix of entertainment and information. The shops allow visitors to browse, learn, and buy while exploring state-of-the-art, museum-quality displays on natural history, science, and technology. CORE was commissioned to design the 2,000-square-foot Discovery Channel store at Pittsburgh International Airport, a shop that focuses on travel, adventure, and aviation.

CORE used a visual and tactile palette that focuses on materials in their natural state, reinforcing the Discovery Channel's identity as an exploratory medium. The poured concrete-slab floor, colored green and blue, suggests the topography of land and water masses on a map or globe. The drywall/wallboard wall surfaces have a rough skip-trowel finish, creating the illusion of stone or sand. The tensile fabric canopies above the display fixtures are wispy and cloud-like, while blue uplighting on the exposed ceiling alludes to the sky.

CORE developed simple and flexible display fixtures as a kit of parts. Standard steel pipe, scaffold fittings, metal pegboards, and a variety of display-surface sizes and shapes can be easily reconfigured to accommodate an ever-changing product assortment.

The horizontal shelves are constructed of clear glass, translucent glass, medium density fiberboard, and recycled plastic, all of which allow light to penetrate the upper portions of the fixture and filter down through the shelves, all the way to the bottom. Above the perimeter fixture, a light canopy made of spandex tensile fabric reflects light back down into the store. The canopy illuminates the upper levels of the fixture, while ceiling fixtures outside of the canopy light the lower portion.

Display fixtures are a kit of parts, including standard steel pipe, scaffold fittings, metal pegboards, and a variety of display surface sizes and shapes. CORE custom designed the system to accommodate a changing assortment of products.

EXPLORE
OUR WORLD

The 2,000-square-foot store incorporates state-of-the-art technology, which allows shoppers to browse, learn, and explore in the museum-quality environment.

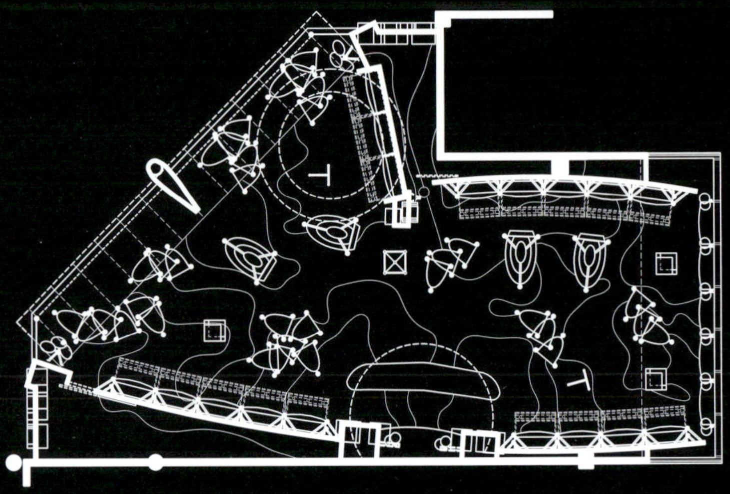

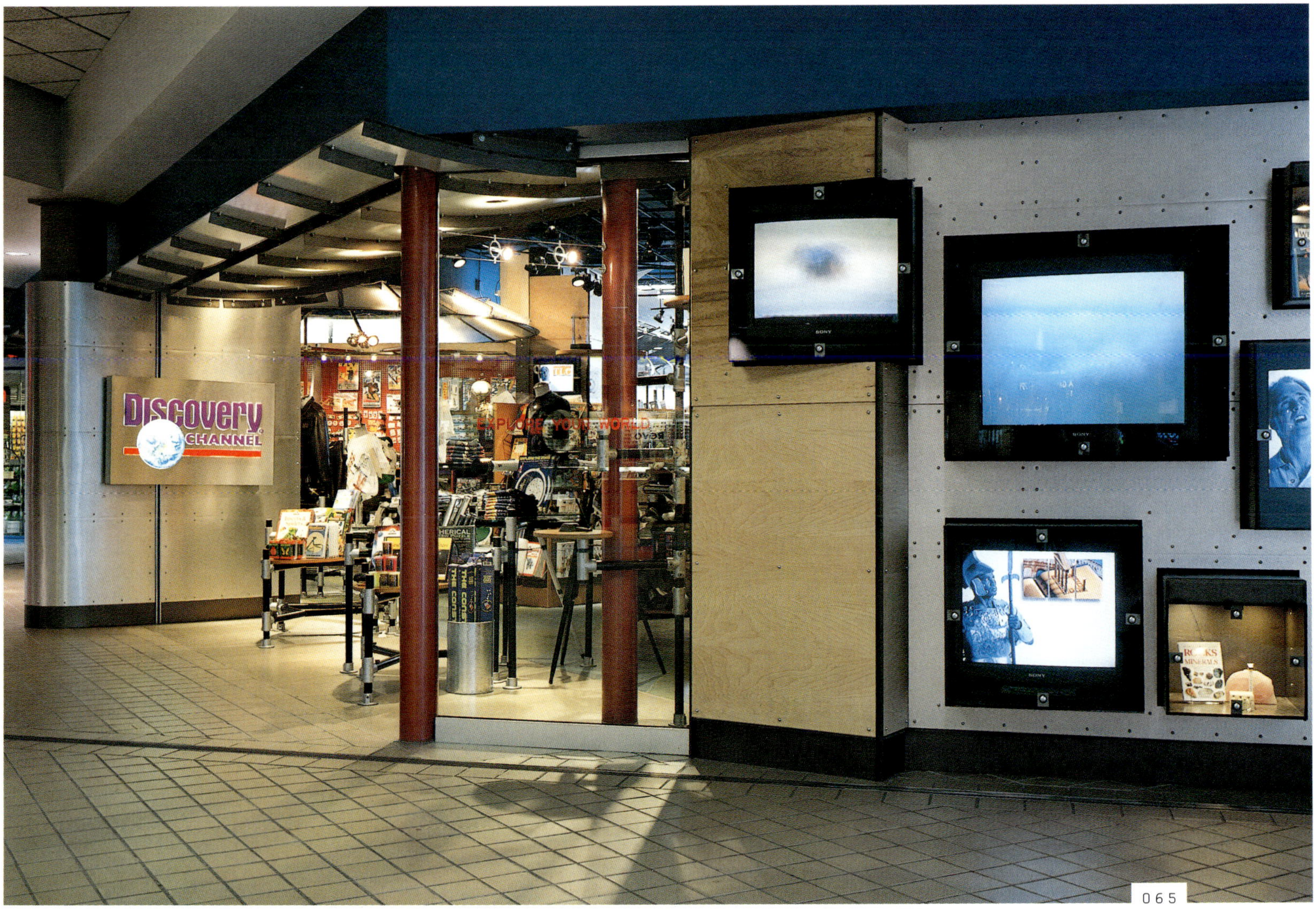

CORE focused on materials that relate to the Discovery Channel's exploration of the natural world. Poured green and blue concrete-slab floors, wall surfaces with a skip-trowel finish, and fabric canopies allude to land and water masses, sand and stone, and open sky.

EA

DEAN & DELUCA: MARKETHOUSE

Washington, DC 1992

"The store must appear as though it's been here for a hundred years, and when we leave in a hundred years, no one should ever know we've been here." This was CORE's mission for the renovation and restoration of the Markethouse in Georgetown, Washington, DC. The structure was originally built in 1802 and has undergone subsequent additions and renovations. It originally functioned as a market but has also been a food court and an automobile parts store. Since the building has great historical significance, the architects took special care while incorporating the technically complex program.

A new standing seam roof, which accommodates the building's elaborate mechanical and exhaust needs, matches the original structure. Thousands of feet of concealed conduit and piping run under the floor to the equipment. The floor itself was not attached to the building walls in order to preserve the existing historic structure. CORE carefully controlled the location and form of all exposed utility services, bringing the facility into compliance with ADA regulations.

The 40-foot main façade facing M Street features three 15-foot arched bays. The central bay is positioned between two large windows and contains the main entryway. The façade's intricately stamped cornice is accented by dentilled and bracketed raking cornices. Round arched window openings are separated by brick pilasters on the exterior.

By adding a canopy structure, the design established an outdoor café area. Service lines for the café run through the foundation wall and the floor slab so that the existing walls are not penetrated. The rest of the exterior remains intact; only the trim and doors underwent minor renovations and received a new coat of paint.

CORE renovated and restored the Markethouse, taking careful steps to preserve the historic exterior details of the 1802 structure while accommodating the Dean & Deluca shop. Only trim and doors underwent minor changes and received a new coat of paint.

DEAN & DELUCA
3276
USA TODAY

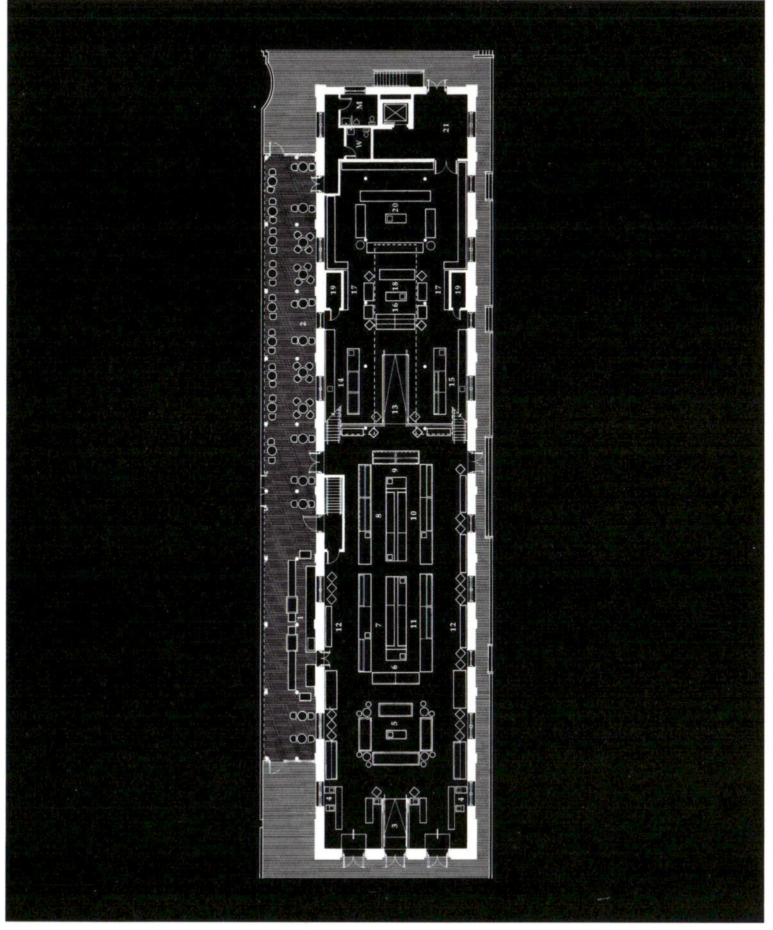

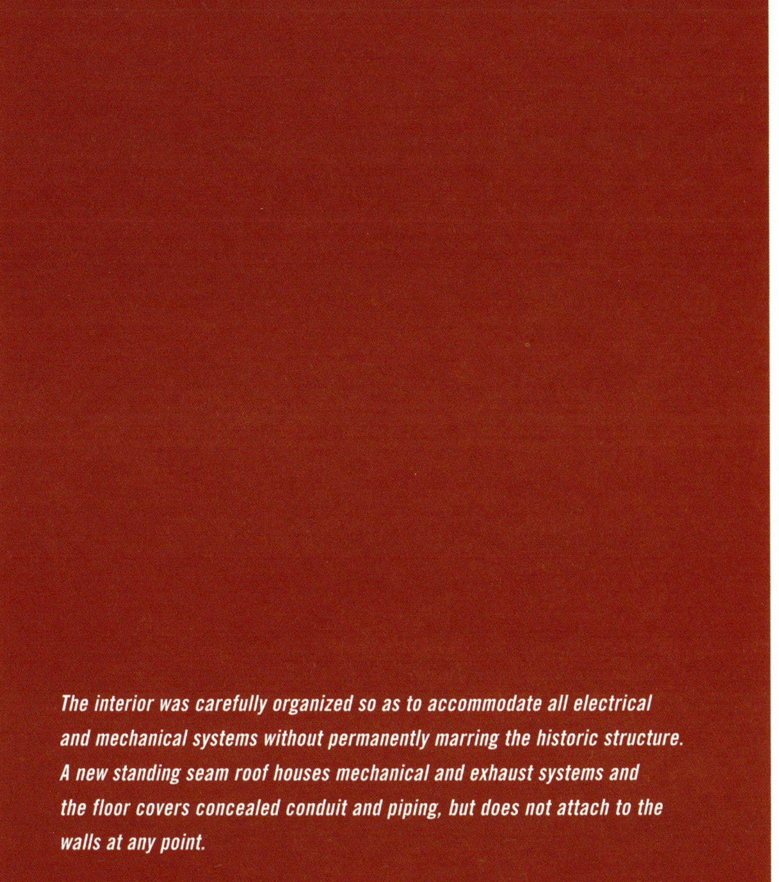

The interior was carefully organized so as to accommodate all electrical and mechanical systems without permanently marring the historic structure. A new standing seam roof houses mechanical and exhaust systems and the floor covers concealed conduit and piping, but does not attach to the walls at any point.

DEAN & DELUCA: WARNER THEATER

Washington, DC 1993

Dean & Deluca gave CORE a straightforward mandate to design a café beneath the historic Warner Theater in downtown Washington, DC. The company requested a store that feels as though it is an extension of the orchestra pit, but with the sparkle of a marquee.

The 56-seat café's peculiar underground location—directly beneath the theater's stage and orchestra pit—presented CORE with many design challenges. The space was located five feet below street level, with its food prep area an additional four feet below the seating area. CORE had to confront several structural obstacles: a series of massive, stepped concrete piers along the perimeter of the space, which support a new building above the theater, and rows of crossbeams supporting the stage and orchestra pit directly overhead. Besides being so imposing and taking up valuable space, the piers and crossbeams limited where CORE could install mechanical and electrical systems.

Rather than fight so many impediments, CORE embraced them and integrated them into their design. They hung mechanical and electrical equipment along and underneath the piers and beams, and treated the exposed structure as a visual pattern that extends across the café. CORE used bright wall finishes, reflective tiles, and high-intensity directional lights, which can be replaced with low voltage lighting fixtures to make the space sparkle like a marquee, as the client requested.

The 56-seat café is located beneath the stage and orchestra pit of the historic Warner Theater. The below grade location created many structural obstacles, such as stepped concrete piers and rows of crossbeams.

CORE utilized the structural impediments in their design, rather than trying to cover them. Mechanical and electrical equipment hang along and underneath the piers and beams, turning the exposed structure into a visual pattern. Details such as bright wall finishes, reflective tiles, and high-intensity lights allude to the glitzy and glamorous performances that take place upstairs.

TYPHOON BREWERY

New York, New York 1996

This project was a gut renovation of an existing space, occupying two floors of an early 20th-century row house and part of a contiguous 45-story high-rise, into a restaurant and on-site brewery. CORE's sleek design focuses on the visual excitement of the brewing process and equipment.

CORE removed a large part of the second floor of the townhouse, creating a dramatic two-story space edged along one side by a wall of glass-enclosed beer tanks. A new glass and steel façade inserted into the existing building's stone exterior exposes the tanks to the street. One of the biggest challenges was accommodating this brewing equipment, which would take up 2,200 square feet of the 12,000-square-foot restaurant. The process required eight serving tanks, eight fermenting and conditioning tanks, and two 15-barrel brewhouse tanks, each of which weighs 400 pounds empty and 3,000 pounds full. CORE separated the brewing area from the dining room and connected them with a painted steel bridge that provides access to the brewmaster.

A glass and steel canopy hangs over the entry vestibule, which is finished in muted, galvanized metal. The interior boasts honed slate tabletops, a stainless steel raw bar, and dropped ceilings of patinated galvanized metal. To prevent excessive noise and echo from so many hard surfaces, the designers used wall-to-wall carpeting throughout the space.

An L-shaped exhibition kitchen with bright ochre-colored ceramic tiles dominates the dining room. Customers can pull up cast aluminum and cherry wood stools to a counter with a view of the chef. CORE removed the original space's non-structural interior partitions and replaced the second floor ceiling with a partially deconstructed one to increase light and views throughout the interior.

CORE gutted two floors of an early 20th-century row house and part of a contiguous high-rise to accommodate this restaurant with its on-site brewery. A new glass and steel façade reveals the brewing tanks to passersby.

Brewery
Brewery
22

CORE used metallic finishes to create a sleek, modern aesthetic. A glass
and steel canopy, which hangs over the entry vestibule, is finished in muted,
galvanized metal. The two-story restaurant features a stainless steel raw
bar and dropped ceilings of patinated galvanized metal.

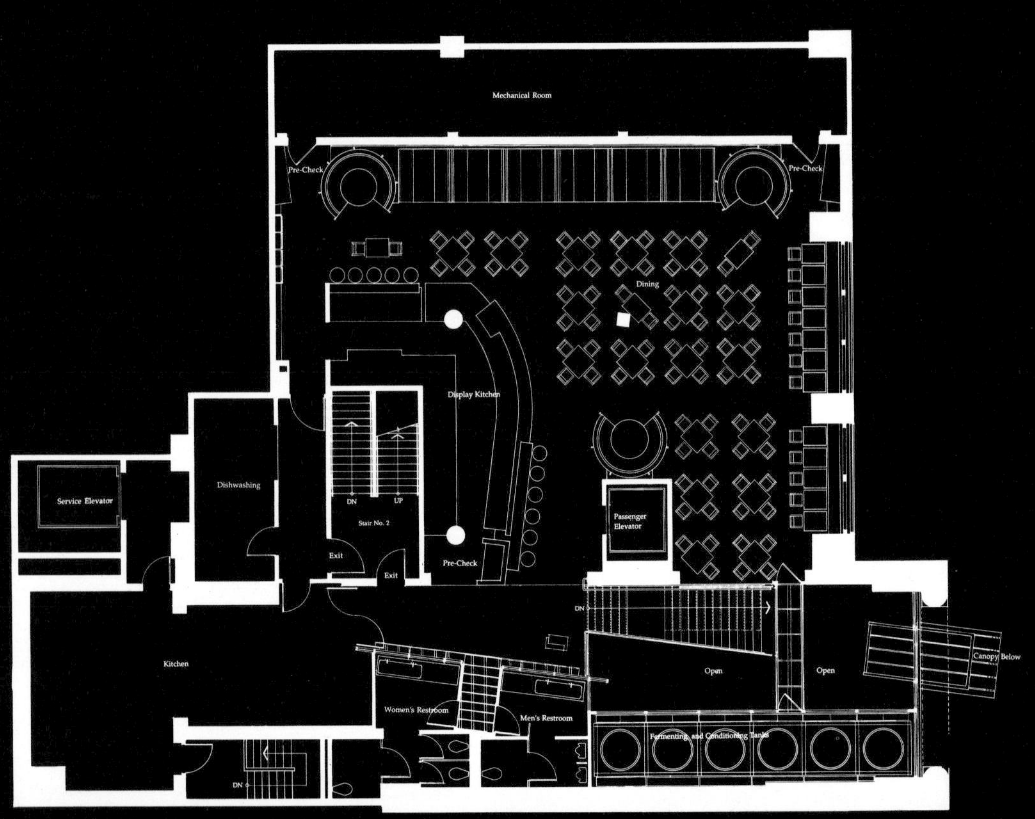

Stair No. 2
UP
DN
UP
UP
Service Elevator
Passenger Elevator
Stair No. 1
DN
Exit
Exit
Exit
Exit
Coats
UP
Entry
Satay Bar
Pick-up
Bar
Bar
Brewing Area
UP
DN
Stair No. 3

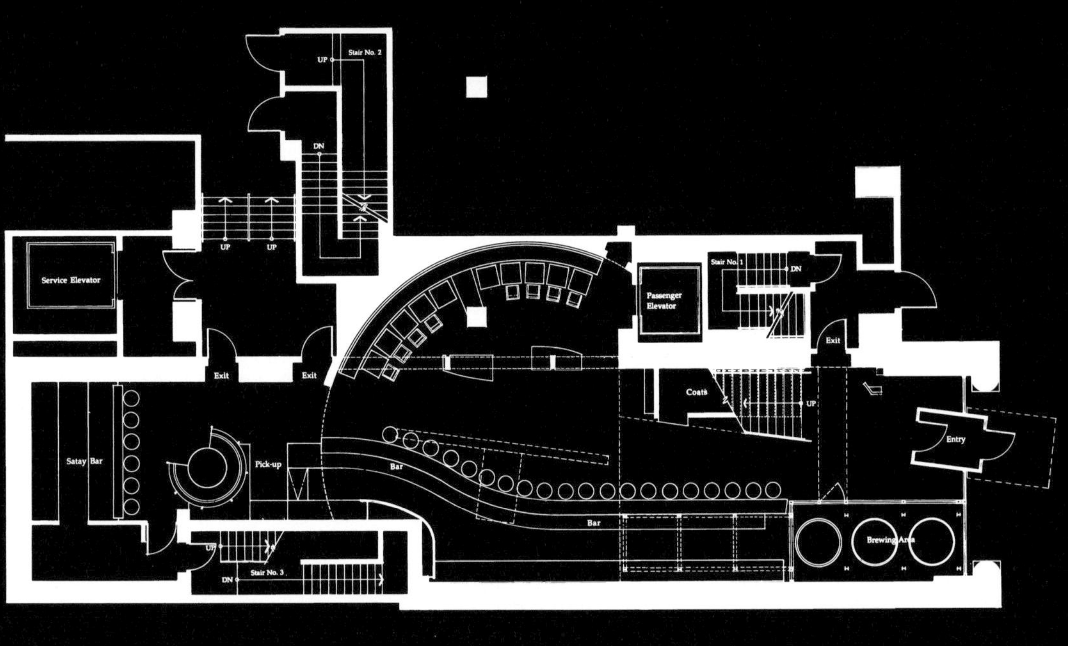

Mechanical Room
Pre-Check
Pre-Check
Dining
Display Kitchen
Service Elevator
Dishwashing
DN
UP
Stair No. 2
Passenger Elevator
Exit
Exit
Pre-Check
DN
Kitchen
Open
Open
Canopy Below
Women's Restroom
Men's Restroom
Fermenting and Conditioning Tanks
DN

CORE separated the brewing area from the dining room and connected them
with a painted steel bridge that provides access to the brewmaster.
Non-structural interior partitions were replaced with partially deconstructed
partitions, which increase light and views throughout the interior.

HANNIBAL'S

College Park, Maryland 1996

The Hannibal's chain of coffeehouses is the first of a new breed of cafés that rely on the image of existing space to establish its identity. CORE used open ceilings, pendant light fixtures, and large windows to re-create the open-air atmosphere of Parisian outdoor cafés.

CORE chose blue-tiled walls and cherry wood countertops to create a quiet mood that would draw customers into a relaxed and casual atmosphere. Bar seating along the windows and a lounge with magazine racks makes Hannibal's attractive to both busy customers with little time to spend, and the patrons who want to spend a leisurely afternoon at the café. CORE included ample shelf space where students could store their books and papers while relaxing.

CORE completely gutted the existing space, originally the back of a Roy Rogers restaurant and a CVS drugstore, and installed all new electrical, mechanical, and plumbing systems. They kept the cracked concrete floor to evoke a well-worn, industrial aesthetic. CORE pulled the feeling of the street inside the coffeehouse with raw materials such as wood, glass, metal, and concrete, which they integrated into the service counter, lighting fixtures, condiment stations, and seating areas to create Hannibal's image.

CORE used large windows in the façade of this coffee shop to create an open-air atmosphere akin that of a Parisian café.

HANNIBAL'S
COFFEE
HANNIBAL'S
COFFEE
HANNIBAL'S
COFFEE
LEASING

CORE completely gutted the inside of this former drugstore and restaurant, using raw materials, such as wood, glass, metal, and concrete to relate to the street and create Hannibal's well-worn, industrial aesthetic.

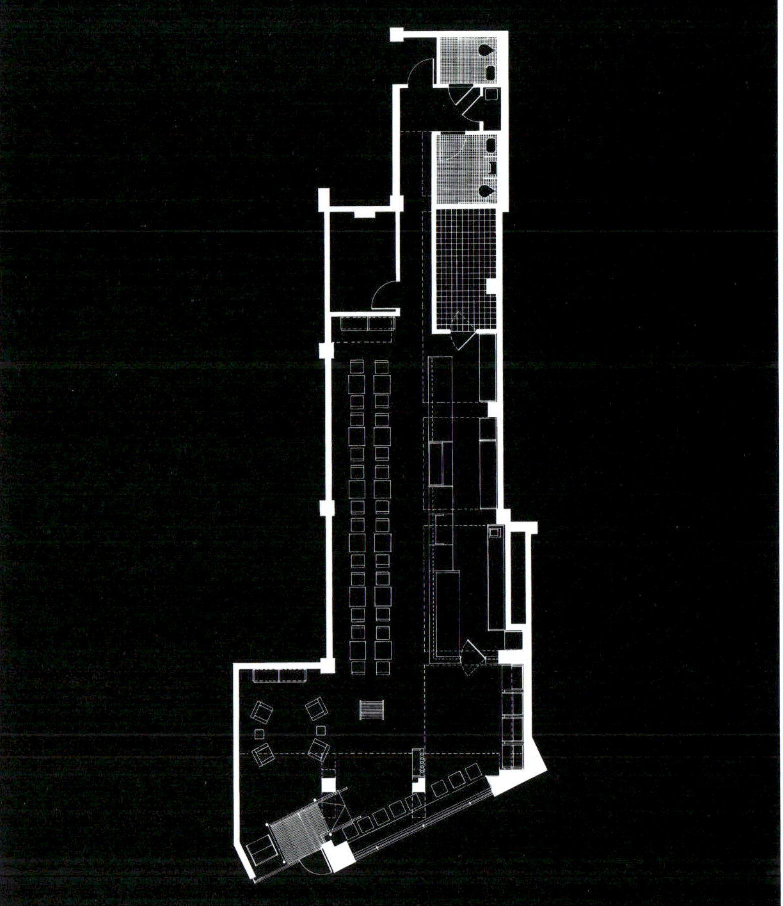

BREADLINE

Washington, DC 1997

CORE let innovative, budget-conscious design drive the plans for an upscale yet non-traditional bakery and restaurant located half a block from the White House. Given its location, the 3,500-square-foot shop, which specializes in fresh baked goods sold in a fast-food format, had to appeal to tourists as well as 9-to-5-ers from the surrounding downtown office district.

CORE's design, assisted by baker/owner Mark Furstenburg, focused on the bread-making process within the aptly named Breadline. The space includes an open kitchen that exposes the baking process to customers. CORE even designed the ceiling panels, composed of drywall and perforated lay-in access panels, in bread-shaped forms and designated the walls opposite the bakery as a photo gallery, which displays images of people baking bread and enjoying good food.

CORE divided the seating in this area into two levels. One level features bar-height seating directly across from the grill. Diners can see over the counter to the activity at the grill. Customers have views of the bakery from another seating area with standard-height tables. Lightbulbs of various sizes and shapes, suspended from cords of varying lengths, compromise the lighting system. The architects kept costs down by exposing assembled hardware and mechanical systems and choosing rougher industrial finishes. There are some custom elements, including millwork and furniture, but these are minimalist—and kept to a minimum.

With a palette of mustard yellow, olive green, and rust orange, Breadline has a warm, bright, and inviting atmosphere. There's a homey feeling conveyed by the quilted stain pattern of the concrete floor, the uneven grain of the wood paneling, and the striped tile patterns behind the kitchen.

This upscale bakery and restaurant, located half a block from the White House, needed a refined design that would appeal to professionals, as well as tourists. CORE used an earthy palette to create a warm, inviting atmosphere.

The grill and bakery are exposed so that customers can watch as their food is prepared. Seating is available at a bar opposite the grill and at standard tables.

EXIT
EXIT

FAIRMONT BAR & DINING

Bethesda, Maryland 1999

This restaurant in Bethesda is establishing itself as a neighborhood eatery with loyal customers. Fashioned after establishments such as the Union Square Café in New York, this restaurant focuses as much on food as it does on service. The vision for Fairmont Bar & Dining was born of a distinct view of how far contemporary restaurants have come, and how far they have gotten away from the original taverns, which were places where the community came together to socialize.

The restaurant features window seating overlooking Fairmont Avenue. A large bar incorporates monitors for viewing sports and classic movies. Seating includes a 20-person private dining room, a main dining room that seats 60, and a 12-person community table. The open kitchen, located adjacent to the community table, is visible from the entire restaurant.

An earth-tone palette features highlight colors, which reflect the four seasons. The atmosphere created by this palette is bolstered with other design elements, such as concrete floors, mahogany booths, and a steel-topped bar. The pale celery-colored ceiling is composed of various elevations and a mahogany arbor element over the four circular booths.

In their design for this restaurant, CORE took care to establish a neighborhood eatery that would attract loyal customers and promote a tavern-like atmosphere. Windows in the façade connect the restaurant to Fairmont Avenue.

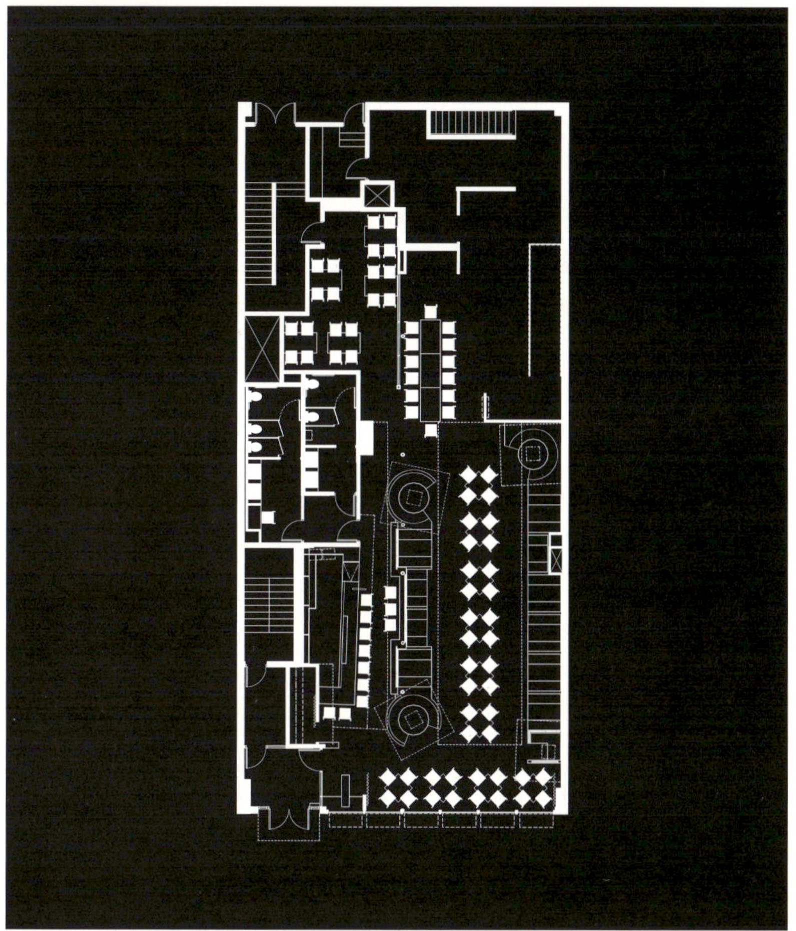

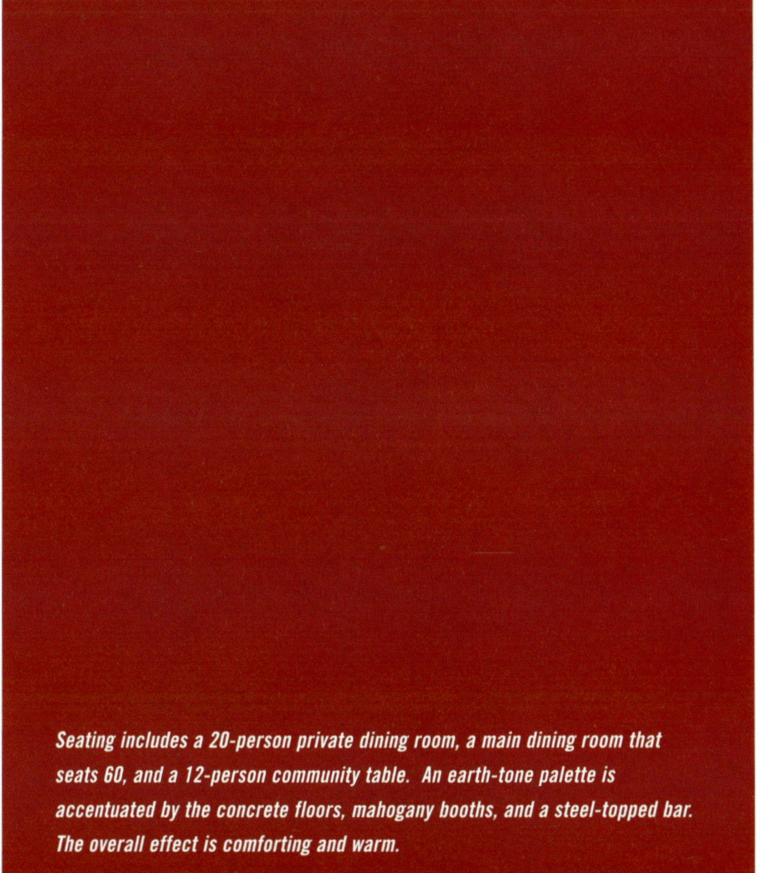

Seating includes a 20-person private dining room, a main dining room that seats 60, and a 12-person community table. An earth-tone palette is accentuated by the concrete floors, mahogany booths, and a steel-topped bar. The overall effect is comforting and warm.

GREENWOOD

Washington, DC 2001

Greenwood restaurant is a stark departure from the formal dining experiences of the Washington, DC, area. The 85-seat dining room and bar occupy a 20-foot-wide section of a street, fronted by an urban strip center designed in the 40's. CORE reorganized the space, which was previously an Indian restaurant, but left the kitchen shell and an existing wood-burning grill intact.

CORE and chef/owner Carole Greenwood created a community dining experience with a 22-seat shared table prominently located in the center of the dining room. A bar to the right of the entry flanks the community table and 2- and 4-person tables are organized around the remaining edges of the dining room.

CORE focused on a handcrafted aesthetic and incorporated the work of a local artist to connect the concept and the space to the community. The artist Colby Caldwell's handwaxed photographic series adorns the wall behind the limestone-topped bar, establishing a tranquil setting. The coloring of the photographs works well with the restaurant's overall color palette. CORE exposed the original stamped tin ceiling of the 1930s building and also left a simple lath ceiling that had been used to support a suspended ceiling. The exposed mechanical ductwork is neatly tucked against the edges of the space. Custom, blown-glass lamps hang at several different levels throughout the restaurant, providing general illumination and accenting the rich colors and soft glow of the artwork.

CORE incorporated familiar yet sophisticated materials, textures, and colors to create a quiet, comfortable atmosphere for diners. Millwork crafted from rough-cut, salvaged wood was left unfinished to bring out the weathered texture of the material. The walls were treated with several layers of varying shades of red paint to create a weathered appearance. Meanwhile, a new plane-sliced hardwood floor gives a clean feel to the space.

For Geenwood restaurant, CORE established a handcrafted aesthetic, using the handwaxed photographic series of local artist Colby Caldwell, as well as custom hand-blown lamps.

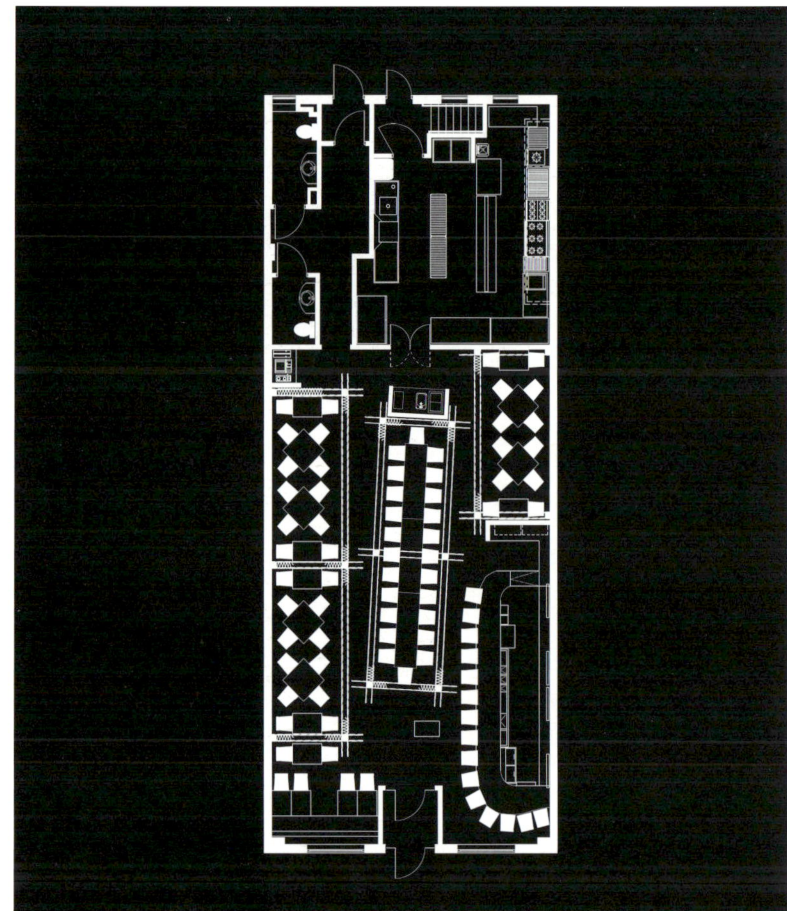

CORE completely reorganized the space, a 20-foot-wide section of a street, fronted by a strip center designed in the '40s, but left the kitchen shell and an existing wood-burning grill intact. A community dining table occupies the center of the space A bar sits to the right of the community table and 2- and 4-person tables are organized at the perimeter of the space.

CORE used rustic, but sophisticated materials, such as rough-cut, salvaged wood millwork and a new plane-sliced hardwood floor. These details combine with the weathered red walls and the artwork to create a quiet, comfortable atmosphere for diners.

CORE CREDITS

A&E 1400 Currency Drive, San Antonio, Texas. **CONTRACTOR**: Del Greco Construction Services. **CLIENT**: A&E Signature Services. **BBC AMERICA** 7473 Wisconsin Avenue, 11th Floor, Bethesda, Maryland. **DATE**: 1998. **CONTRACTOR**: JGM Construction. **CLIENT**: BBC America. **BREADLINE** 1751 Pennsylvania Avenue, NW, Washington, DC. **DATE**: 1997. **CONTRACTOR**: Kerr Mast. **ENGINEER**: Metropolitan Engineering Inc. **FOOD SERVICE**: Next Step Design. **GRAPHIC DESIGN**: Thrust. **MILLWORK**: Enterprise Woodcraft & Design, Inc. **CLIENT**: Breadline. **CATHOLIC CHARITIES** 924 G Street, NWm Washington, DC 20001. **CONTRACTOR**: D&M Construction, Inc. **CLIENT**: Catholic Charities. **DEAN & DELUCA: MARKETHOUSE** Georgetown, 3276 M Street, NW, Washington, DC. **DATE**: 1992. **CONTRACTOR**: Donohoe Construction Co., Inc. **ELECTRICAL ENGINEER**: Walter C. Davis & Sons, Inc. **KITCHEN**: Kitchen Consultants, Inc. **MECHANICAL ENGINEER**: Girard Engineering, Ltd. **REFRIGERATION**: Richmond Refrigeration. **STRUCTURAL ENGINEER**: Cagley & Associates. **CLIENT**: Dean & Deluca. **DEAN & DELUCA: WARNER THEATER** 1299 Pennsylvania Avenue, NW, Washington, DC. **DATE**: 1993. **CONTRACTOR**: Donohoe Construction Co., Inc. **KITCHEN**: Kitchen Consultants, Inc. **MECHANICAL ENGINEER**: Girard Engineering, Ltd. **REFRIGERATION**: Richmond Refrigeration. **CLIENT**: Dean & Deluca. **DISCOVERY CHANNEL STORE** Central Service Building Midfield Terminal, Pittsburgh International Airport, Pittsburgh, Pennsylvania. **DATE**: 1997. **CONTRACTOR**: Shannon Construction Company. **ELECTRICAL ENGINEER**: Gerso Electric. **MASONRY**: Kein & Son. **PAINT**: Richie Interiors. **WOOD & PLASTICS/FURNISHINGS**: Excell Store Fixtures. **CLIENT**: Discovery Communications, Inc. **E-SYNC** 35 Nutmeg Drive, Trumbull, Connecticut. **DATE**: 2000. **CONTRACTOR**: Scott Thomas Construction, Inc. **CLIENT**: David Teitelman. **FAIRMONT BAR & DINING** 4936 Fairmont Avenue, Bethesda, Maryland. **CONTRACTOR**: Austin Construction Company. **CLIENT**: Bob McKay and Jim Davis. **GREENWOOD** 5031 Connecticut Avenue Washington, DC 20008. **CONTRACTOR**: Kadcon Corporation. **ARTWORK**: Colby Caldwell. **FURNITURE**: Gar Products. **LIGHTING**: Dagget Glass Studio. **MILLWORK**: Han's Construction. **CLIENT**: Carole Greenwood. **HANNIBAL'S** 7300-B Baltimore Avenue, College Park, Maryland. **CONTRACTOR**: The J.R. Austin Company. **FOOD SERVICE**: Next Step Design Group. **LIGHTING**: Moran Coventry Lighting Associates. **MEP**: Face Associates, Inc. **MILLWORK**: Enterprise Woodcraft & Design. **CLIENT**: Hannibal's.

N.E.W. CUSTOMER SERVICE COMPANIES, INC. First Avenue North, Great Falls, Montana. **DATE:** 1998. **CONTRACTOR:** Dick Anderson Construction, Inc. **CLIENT:** N.E.W. Customer Service Companies, Inc. **NATIONAL MINORITY AIDS COUNCIL** 1931 & 1933 13th Street, NW, Washington, DC. **DATE:** 1995. **CONTRACTOR:** Malin Construction, Inc. **MEP:** Face Associates, Inc. **STRUCTURAL ENGINEER:** Rathgeber/Goss Associates. **CLIENT:** National Minority AIDS Council. **PORTER NOVELLI** 1120 Connecticut Avenue, NW, Washington, DC. **DATE:** 1993. **CONTRACTOR:** Blake Construction. **ENGINEER:** Girard Engineering, Ltd. **LIGHTING:** Moran Coventry Lighting Associates. **MILLWORK:** Enterprise Woodcraft & Design. **CLIENT:** Porter/Novelli. **PORTER NOVELLI: INTERACTIVE** The Millennium, 1909 K Street, NWm Washington, DC 20036. **CONTRACTOR:** StructureTone, Inc. **FURNITURE:** Steelcase. **MOVER:** Moving Details. **CLIENT:** Porter/Novelli. **PROFUMI** White Flint Mall, 11301 Rockville Pike, North Bethesda, Maryland. **DATE:** 1994. **CONTRACTOR:** Malin Construction, Inc. **LIGHTING:** Moran Coventry Lighting Associates. **METAL:** Dameron Forge. **MILLWORK:** Enterprise Woodcraft & Design. **CLIENT:** Profumi. **SMARTEAM** 1612 U Street, NW, Suite 401, Washington, DC. **DATE:** 1998. **CONTRACTOR:** Artistic Design Build Inc. **ELECTRICAL ENGI-NEERING:** Mr. Electric Inc. **FINISHES:** Shaw Commercial. **FURNISHINGS:** De Young & Associates. **SPECIALTIES:** Cascade Coil Drapery; Henderson. **HARDWARE, WOOD & PLASTICS:** Nature's Waye Woodworking. **CLIENT:** Smarteam Communications Inc. **APC/SPRINT PCS STORE** 1908/1911 Chain Bridge Road, Tysons Corner, Virginia **DATE:** 1995. **CONTRACTOR:** J.R. Austin. **LIGHTING:** Moran Coventry Lighting Associates. **MEP:** Face Associates, Inc. **MILLWORK:** Enterprise Woodcraft & Design, Inc. **STRUCTURAL ENGINEER:** Rathgeber/Goss Associates. **CLIENT:** American Personal Communications. **TYPHOON BREWERY** 22 East 54th Street, New York, New York. **DATE:** 1996. **CONTRACTOR:** M.A. Angeliades, Inc. **FOOD SERVICE:** Next Step Design. **FURNITURE:** Knossos Furniture. **LIGHTING:** Moran Coventry Lighting Associates. **MEP:** Atkinson Koven Feinberg Engineers, LLP. **METAL:** Thomas Hand Architectural Metals. **STRUCTURAL ENGINEER:** Rathgeber/Goss Associates. **CLIENT:** Strafford Ventures.

PHOTOGRAPHY **BREADLINE** by Maxwell MacKenzi. **DISCOVERY CHANNEL STORE** by Michael Moran and Kevin R. Cooke. **ALL OTHER PROJECTS** by Michael Moran.

ACKNOWLEDGEMENTS

Envisioning a firm committed to working with others concerned with the quality of their environment and the importance of design, we created CORE on August 1, 1991. We set out not just to achieve great design, but to achieve it in new and better ways. We pursue creativity and innovation in every aspect of our work, because successful projects meet more than physical requirements.

Individually we define and emphasize personal and professional values differently. There is no denying, however, that our values are more than ideals; they are the reason the firm exists. They are high standards that make our work more meaningful and more enjoyable. Our designs embody our values, not the shock of the new. We value functional innovation over experiments or flights of fancy.

Great design requires teamwork and an open relationship between client and designer. Our team approach and emphasis on flexibility and innovation create an integrated strategy for design that transcends outdated notions of "service" and culminates in a commitment to completing the work. This entails managing and communicating our ideas until the project is done right.

Design is the thoughtful creation and manipulation of space. We design with a simple, continual aspiration to create, to combine ideas in new ways, and to do so with a strong sense of aesthetic integrity that is appropriate, pragmatic, and original. To us, design is a mysterious blend of creativity, pragmatism, style, cost, and detail. It is the ceaseless aspiration to create made tangible.

When we established CORE we could not have anticipated what lay ahead. We have experienced success, failure, and, most importantly, acknowledgement. We would not have received this acknowledgement without family, staff, patrons, clients, and consultants, all too numerous to mention. They have all been patient and understanding. They have believed in us. Our vision has lead us down many paths and produced a vast portfolio. This book contains only a small portion of our work. We are thankful to everyone who has come through our door and been a part of our journey-especially our wives, Jan and Sallie.

We are incredibly fortunate to work with several individuals who have become an extension of our firm. It takes creative diligence to focus our tangents. Michael Moran has almost exclusively photographed our work. It is his eye that sees what we have created and captures it in time. Dan Snyder has been a great client and mentor. Chuck Seelye at Trust and Kate Damon at Kaze have invented and reinvented our identity and brand. Maureen Moran has repeatedly lighted us up. Deborah Dietsch has been a great motivator. Brent Nelson and Mike Sayers have kept the technology flowing. Randy Estabrook is an extraordinary millworker. We are incredibly thankful. — *Peter F. Hapstak III, AIA, IIDA, ISP and Dale A. Stewart, AIA*

STAFF

Thomas Aaron, John Abraham, Ghassan Abukurah, Robyn Amos, Richard Anderson,
Peter Anna, David Arwood, Parinaz Bahadori, Deletra Bailey, Quito Banogon,
Jeff Barber, Clay Batchelor, Brian Berger, Lidia Berger, Tony Beto, Susan Block,
Chris Blomquist, Aimee Boyer, Lou Boza, David Braun, Andrew Bray, Robert Burns,
Anja Caldwell, Brian Calis, Brent Campbell, Cynthia Camp, Christina Carpio,
Robin Cary, Maria Casarella, I-Hsing Chao, Bryan Chun, Alisha Clark,
Robert Cole, Alex Coleman, Leigh Ann Coleman, Dawn Congdon, Jerry Conrad,
David Conrath, Kevin Coyne, Kelly Cragle, Julie Cueto, Cassandra Cullison,
Joy Dean, Richard Deane, William Deegan, Jeffrey Deffenbaugh, Jose Deynes,
Debra Dionesotes, Carolyn Donnelly, Nancy Doran, Jennifer Fagan, Teresa Fallen,
Ken Farrell, Leah Faulk, Sean Finn, David Fowler, Bob Fox, Melissa Francis,
Michael Francis, Jerry Freeman, Gary Friedman, Regina Gilbert, Amy Giller,
Nathaniel Ginsburg, Scott Gordon, Bill Greeves, Spencer Grice, Jesse Guerra,
Kendra Guiffre, Vyt Gureckas, Randy Guseman, Laya Hague, Kendra Hamilton,
Soho Hancock, Faisal Hassan, Kevin Hayes, Lisa Henderson, Mia Hill,
Holly Hollmeyer, Diana Horvat, Cynthia Hough, Pauline Ingram, Maralyn Jones,
David Kay, Greg Keffer, Scott Klugel, David Ko, Meryl Kramer, Erika Lehman,
Jennifer Leonard, Bob Leonhardt, Rodrigo Letonja, Michele LeTourneur,
Oy Bill Lieu, Norlie Lin, Karen Lloyd, Daun Longshore, Tony Maher,
Ajmal Maiwandi, Patricia Mao, Stephanie Marcello, Margret McConnell,
Keith Mehner, Joel Meneses, Jaymee Messler, Brian Miller, Jason Miller,
Jose Monzon, Katarzyna Mroczek, John Musolino, Kathleen Ngiam, Scott Nguyen,
Barbara Noguera, Michael Noll, Celie Norton, Steve Ollis, Jiyun Park,
Laurie Kohn Parkinson, John Paull, Shari Perago, Brent Pfister, Lee Powell,
Tomas Quijano, Pablo Quintana, Adriana Radulescu, Sherry Ray, Alastair Reilly,
Regina Reilly, Maria Riano, Patricia Richardson, Kim Riley, Mark Rowan,
Abosede Rufai, Joanie Rufo, Meredith Sabol, Ramon Santos, Bruce Saunders,
Marc Schneiderman, Brian Scull, Christian Seitz, Randy Seitz, Patricia Shaker,
Stephanie Shapard, Bruce Shirley, Bernardo Siles, Katherine Smith,
Katherine Snider, Susan Stine, Colleen Stone, Kimberly Strickland, Sofia Vitkin,
Domagoj Vokic, Robert Vorkapich, Tibor Wagner, Desta Wallace, Esther Wong,
Sean Wayne, Apryl Webb, Kathleen Webber, Carl Westerman,
Christine (Wan) Williams, Ken Wilson, Rob Wilson, Jason Wilt, Abby Wittman,
Tom Womeldurf, Christina Wright, Doris Yeo, Connie Zalduondo, Mark Zweifel.